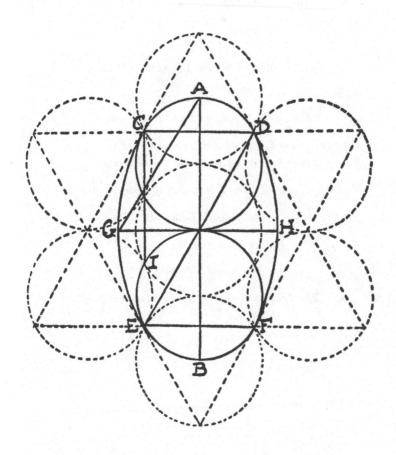

KEY OF THE COSMOS AND NUMBERS

P C
1927

THE TAROT

A Key to the Wisdom of the Ages

THE TAROT

A Key to the Wisdom of the Ages

THE CLASSIC GUIDE BY

PAUL FOSTER CASE

JEREMY P. TARCHER · PENGUIN
a member of Penguin Group (USA) Inc.
New York
2006

JEREMY P. TARCHER / PENGUIN
Published by the Penguin Group
Penguin Group (USA) Inc., 375 Hudson Street, New York, New York 10014, USA · Penguin Group
(Canada), 90 Eglinton Avenue East, Suite 700, Toronto, Ontario M4P 2Y3, Canada (a division of Pearson
Penguin Canada Inc.) · Penguin Books Ltd, 80 Strand, London WC2R 0RL, England · Penguin Ireland,
25 St Stephen's Green, Dublin 2, Ireland (a division of Penguin Books Ltd) · Penguin Group (Australia),
250 Camberwell Road, Camberwell, Victoria 3124, Australia (a division of Pearson Australia Group Pty
Ltd) · Penguin Books India Pvt Ltd, 11 Community Centre, Panchsheel Park, New Delhi–110 017, India
Penguin Group (NZ), Cnr Airborne and Rosedale Roads, Albany, Auckland 1310, New Zealand
(a division of Pearson New Zealand Ltd) · Penguin Books (South Africa) (Pty) Ltd,
24 Sturdee Avenue, Rosebank, Johannesburg 2196, South Africa

Penguin Books Ltd, Registered Offices: 80 Strand, London WC2R 0RL, England

First edition published 1947 by Macoy Publishing Company; revised edition published 1990
by Builders of the Adytum; first paperback edition published 2006 by Tarcher/Penguin

Most Tarcher/Penguin books are available at special quantity discounts for bulk purchase for sales
promotions, premiums, fund-raising, and educational needs. Special books or book excerpts also can
be created to fit specific needs. For details, write Penguin Group (USA) Inc. Special Markets, 375
Hudson Street, New York, NY 10014.

Library of Congress Cataloging-in-Publication Data
Case, Paul Foster, 1884–1954.
The tarot : a key to the wisdom of the ages/the classic guide by Paul Foster Case.—1st pbk. ed.
p.   cm.
Originally published: Los Angeles, Calif. : Builders of the Adytum,
Temple of Tarot and Holy Qabalah, c1990.
Includes bibliographical references and index.
ISBN   1-58542-491-9
1. Tarot. I. Title.
BF1879.T2C32   2006   2005055988
133.3'2424—dc22

Printed in the United States of America
3   5   7   9   10   8   6   4   2

While the author has made every effort to provide accurate telephone numbers and Internet addresses
at the time of publication, neither the publisher nor the author assumes any responsibility for errors,
or for changes that occur after publication. Further, the publisher does not have any control over and
does not assume any responsibility for author or third-party websites or their content.

PREFACE TO FIRST REVISED EDITION

THIS IS the first revised edition of Paul Foster Case's classic, *The Tarot, a Key to the Wisdom of the Ages*, since its initial publication in 1947 by Macoy Publishing Company. Over the years, this book has come to be regarded as the seminal work on the Tarot and on the Tarot's intimate connections with Qabalah, Astrology, Alchemy and the other Hermetic Sciences. The only revisions that have been made to the original work are the correction of misspelled words and obvious errors.

Case first began the study of the Tarot in 1900 at the age of sixteen. In 1907 he published the attributions of the Tarot Keys to the letters of the Hebrew alphabet set forth in this book, which attributions he had arrived at as a result of his personal studies. Throughout the early part of this century, Case lectured and published works on the Tarot, Qabalah, Astrology, Alchemy, Masonry, Rosicrucianism and the effect these sciences had on the founding of the United States of America. His work brought him into contact with such persons as Alice Bailey, Michael Whitty, Claude Bragdon, Judge Troward and other leading occultists of that era.

In 1920 Case published *An Introduction to the Study of the Tarot*, now out of print, which was the precursor to this book. In 1922 he published *The Book of Tokens*, a series of twenty-two inspirationally received meditations on the letters of the Hebrew alphabet. In 1929 he published the first edition of *The True and Invisible Rosicrucian Order*, which demonstrated that the original Rosicrucian documents could not be accurately interpreted without a thorough understanding of Qabalah and Tarot, and that true Rosicrucianism was simply the expression of the tenderness of true Christianity.

Throughout this period of time and up until his death, Case was busy preparing detailed lesson material on each aspect of the Western Mystery training system which in his published works he was only able to briefly touch upon. In 1939, Case organized the Builders of the Adytum as an Order dedicated to the perpetuation of the Western Mysteries through the dispensation of these lesson materials in a series of correspondence courses beginning with simple metaphysics and working up through an in-depth study of the Tarot, the Qabalah, the Tree of Life, Gematria, Sound and Color, Alchemy and Astrology. Finally, in 1947, Case was able to publish the present work, which constituted the summation of over forty-five years of study and effort and which represented his magnum opus with respect to the Tarot. Under Case's instruction, artist Jessie Burns Parke (1889–1964) drew the images of the Keys.

It is with gratification and great pleasure that the Stewards of the Order that Case founded announce the publication of this revised edition of his most influential public work. It is our earnest desire that the availability of this book in its present form will inspire its readers to embark upon the journey that leads to the true Self residing in the heart of each of us.

Readers interested in pursuing further the works of Case and his spiritual successor, Ann Davies, as embodied in the curriculum of the Builders of the Adytum or in obtaining black and white Builders of the Adytum Tarot Keys for coloring may write to:

> Builders of the Adytum
> 5101-05 North Figueroa Street
> Los Angeles, California 90042
> www.bota.org

Under the Shadow of His Wings Whose Name Is Peace,

Builders of the Adytum

A NOTE TO THE READER

Members of Builders of the Adytum (B.O.T.A.) believe it is very important that each individual interested in personal unfoldment through the use of Tarot take the time and make the effort to color his or her own Tarot Keys. In the words of Paul Foster Case,

> When you color your own cards, they take on the character of your personality. They are inseparably linked with you! The attention you must give impresses their patterns upon the cells of your brain – builds the details of the designs into your consciousness. And making the Tarot Keys a part of yourself is one of the most practical secrets of all occultism. It is the necessary foundation for all advanced Tarot practice.

Sets of uncolored Tarot Keys and coloring instructions are available from www.bota.org.

—Builders of the Adytum

CONTENTS

ILLUSTRATIONS

THE TAROT

A Key to the Wisdom of the Ages

THE TAROT

A Key to the Wisdom of the Ages

I

INTRODUCTION

THE TAROT is a pictorial text-book of Ageless Wisdom. From its pages has been drawn inspiration for some of the most important works on occult science published during the last seventy-five years. Its influence on the minds of a few enlightened thinkers may be traced throughout the history of the modern revival of interest in esoteric science and philosophy.

This revival began in 1854 with the publication of Eliphas Levi's *Dogma and Ritual of Transcendental Magic*, first of a series of occult writings in which he names the Tarot as his most important source of information. Eliphas Levi's teaching influenced the work of H. P. Blavatsky and Dr. Anna Kingsford. It has been developed and extended in the circles of French occultism in which "Papus" (Dr. Gerard Encausse) was for long a leading spirit. For English readers it is interpreted in the books of S. L. MacGregor Mathers, Dr. W. Wynn Westcott, Dr. Arthur Edward Waite and others. The works of New Thought writers, especially the essays of Judge Thomas Troward, echo it again and again; and, though Levi himself was a nominal Roman Catholic, his doctrine is utilized by Scottish Rite Masonry in the United States, inasmuch as General Albert Pike's *Morals and Dogma of the Scottish Rite* repeats *verbatim* page after page from the French occultist's *Dogma and Ritual*.

Levi's opinion of the Tarot was very high. He said: "As an erudite Kabalistic book, all combinations of

1

which reveal the harmonies preexisting between signs, letters and numbers, the practical value of the Tarot is truly and above all marvelous. A prisoner devoid of books, had he only a Tarot of which he knew how to make use, could in a few years acquire a universal science, and converse with an unequalled doctrine and inexhaustible eloquence."

The aim of this analysis is to show you how to use the Tarot. A full treatment would require many volumes; but I hope to realize the promise of my title by giving a concise explanation of the general plan of the Tarot, and a brief outline of its meaning. It should be understood, however, that the student must fill in this outline with the results of his own observation and meditation.

Before entering upon a description of the construction and symbolism of this book of occult science, it may be well to say a word as to its history. In the main, I am in agreement with Arthur Edward Waite, who discusses the various theories as to its origin in his *Key to the Tarot*, published in London by Wm. Rider and Sons. Dr. Waite concludes that the Tarot has no exoteric history before the fourteenth century. The oldest examples of Tarot designs now preserved in European museums were probably made about 1390. According to an occult tradition, in which I am inclined to place confidence, the actual date of its invention was about the year 1200 A.D.

The inventors, this tradition avers, were a group of adepts who met at stated intervals in the city of Fez, in Morocco. After the destruction of Alexandria, Fez became the literary and scientific capital of the world. Thither, from all parts of the globe, came wise men of all nations, speaking all tongues. Their conferences were made difficult by differences in language and philosophical terminology. So they hit upon the device of embodying the most important of their doctrines in a book of pictures, whose combinations should depend on the occult harmonies of numbers.

Introduction

Perhaps it was a Chinese adept who suggested the idea, for the Chinese have a proverb, "One picture is worth ten thousand words," and Chinese writing is made up of conventionalized pictures. These pictures express ideas instead of words, so that Chinese, Japanese and Koreans, although they speak more than seven different languages, communicate easily with one another, if only they can read and write.

As a skeleton for their invention the wise men chose the relatively simple system of numbers and letters afforded by the Qabalah, or Secret Wisdom of Israel. This esoteric doctrine, apparently Jewish, was really a development of ideas fundamentally identical with the wisdom taught in the secret schools of China, Tibet and India. Some account of it, therefore, must precede our study of the Tarot itself.

The Hebrew Wisdom

The master-key to the Hebrew wisdom is the "name" translated "Lord" in the Authorized Version of the Bible, and "Jehovah" in the revised versions. It is not really a *name* at all, but rather a verbal, numerical and geometrical formula. In Roman letters corresponding to Hebrew it is spelled IHVH.

This is a noun form derived from a Hebrew verb meaning "to be." Correctly translated, it means "That which was, That which is, That which shall be." THAT, not HE. Thus, it is a perfect verbal symbol for the One Reality — for that Something which has always subsisted behind all forms in the eternity of the past, for that Something which really is behind all the appearances and misunderstandings of the present, for that Something which will be the foundation for all the changing forms of life-expression in the eternity to come.

Never has Ageless Wisdom attempted to define this One Reality. Its inner nature defies analysis, cannot be put

3

within the limits of any formal statement, because the One Reality is infinite. Yet, in every age the report of the wise has been that in the One Something inheres the power to *know*. We say, therefore, that IHVH is a verbal symbol for the Conscious Energy that brings all things and creatures into existence.

The Qabalah classifies all possible operations of this One Energy into four planes, or "worlds." Each plane or world is represented by a letter of IHVH, as follows:

The Archetypal World. This is the world of pure ideas. In the archetypal plane are the root-notions inherent in the innermost nature of the universal Conscious Energy. From these ideas are derived all actual forms of manifestation. For example, the pure idea of a chair is the idea of *sitting*. In that idea, as in all others, is embodied a volition — the will-to-sit. This will-to-sit is the single root-notion behind all possible chair-forms that ever have been, are now, or ever shall be. Thus the archetypal world is seen to be the plane of will-ideas. To it Ageless Wisdom assigns the element of fire, representing universal radiant energy. In IHVH this world and this element are represented by the letter "I."

The Creative World. Here the ideas of the archetypal world are specialized as particular patterns. "Sitting" becomes the mental pattern for some special kind of chair. The Cosmic Energy acting on this plane contains the patterns of all chairs that have been made or thought of in the past, of all existing in the present — but not those as yet unthought of. So with all other patterns of particular forms. To this world Ageless Wisdom assigns the element of water, symbolizing the fluid plasticity of the cosmic mind-stuff. The creative world is represented in IHVH by the first "H."

The Formative World. Here the archetypal ideas, specialized in creative patterns, are brought forth into actual expression. It is the plane of processes, the world of forces behind the veil of physical things. The formative world is that which is now explored by physicists and chemists. It is the world of vibratory activities, and also the astral plane of occultism. Here take place the various kinds of action whereby the Cosmic Energy actualizes its patterns. Ageless Wisdom assigns to this world the element of air, representing the life-energy which wise men everywhere have associated with *breath*. The formative world is represented by "V" in IHVH.

The Material World. This is the plane of the actual forms which affect our physical senses. Here the process of bringing down the idea of sitting, through an operation based on the pattern of a particular chair, is finally completed as the chair itself. This plane corresponds to the element of earth, representing the solidity and tangibility of physical objects. It corresponds to the second "H" in IHVH.

In every one of the four worlds, the Qabalah conceives the operation of ten aspects of the universal Conscious Energy. This idea that all possible aspects of the one Reality may be reduced to a tenfold classification is found in every version of the Ageless Wisdom. Thence arises the esoteric teaching concerning the meaning of numbers. This is a subject almost limitless in its ramifications, but what is needed for Tarot study will be found in the next chapter.

II

OCCULT MEANING OF NUMBERS

IN THIS CHAPTER we shall consider the occult significance of
the numbers from Zero to Ten, with particular reference to
the esoteric meanings of the so-called "Arabic" numerals.
As a matter of fact, these numerals were invented by
Hindu priests, from whom they were borrowed (and slightly altered) by the Arab mathematicians who introduced
them into Europe. The key to the meaning of the numerals
is the diagram which appears as the frontispiece of this
book.

Readers of these pages who are familliar with occult
symbolism will perceive that the basis of the construction of this diagram is the six-pointed star, known as the
"Shield of David" and "The Star of the Macrocosm." Years
ago, one of the Theosophical Masters declared that the
system of six circles, tangent to a central seventh, is a key
to the construction of the cosmos. At that time, the
Master's meaning was not grasped by the student to whom
the statement was made.

I hope the inclusion of this diagram in the front of the
book may stimulate some of my readers to further
research. Want of space forbids my developing the various
details. I shall therefore content myself by saying that this
one diagram is a key to the geometrical construction of the
Great Pyramid, to a very close approximation to the squar-
ing of the circle, to the true occult meaning of the apron
worn by Free Masons, to the correct construction of the
Qabalistic diagram known as the Tree of Life (which has
been called "a key to all things"), and to the proportions of
the mysterious Vault in which the body of the founder of
the Rosicrucian Order is said to have been discovered.
These are but a small selection of the mysteries to which

this one diagram affords a clue. I shall confine myself to its numerical significance.

In Arabic notation all numbers are represented by ten symbols, beginning with 0 and ending with 9. They are thus derived from the diagram:

0. An ellipse, representing the Cosmic Egg, whence come all things. Zero is a symbol of the absence of quality, quantity, or mass. Thus it denotes absolute freedom from every limitation whatever. It is a sign of the infinite and eternal Conscious Energy, itself No-Thing, though manifested in everything. It is That which was, is, and shall be forever; but it is nothing we can name. Boundless, infinitely potential, living light, it is the rootless root of all things, of all activities, of all modes of consciousness. In it are included all imaginable and unimaginable possibilities, but it transcends them all. The Qabalists call it: (a) No-Thing; (b) The Boundless; (c) Limitless Light. Pure Conscious Energy, above and beyond thought, to us it is *Superconsciousness.*

The descending arc of the ellipse, on the reader's left, represents Involution, the "winding-up" process whereby Limitless Light manifests itself in name and form. At B the lowest point of involution is reached in the mineral kingdom.

From B back to A on the right side of the ellipse the ascending arc represents Evolution, the "unwinding" process. From B to F is the arc of evolution in the inorganic world. F to H is the arc of organic development up through plants to animals. H to D is the arc of organic development from the lowest animal to the highest type of human consciousness at point D. Only a few human beings have reached this point, but the race is nearer to it now than ever before. The arc from D to A is that of conscious expression beyond human levels, the evolution of conscious one-ness with the Divine.

Thus the two sides of the ellipse suggest the esoteric

doctrine of Involution or descent, and a corresponding Evolution, or ascent. The ascending arc corresponds to the occult doctrine: "First the stone, then the plant, then the animal, then the man, and at last the god."

1. In the diagram, the number *1* is the vertical line from A to B, connecting the extreme height with the extreme depth. Among the many occult meanings of this number are:

Beginning, initiative, originality, unity, singleness, isolation, and the like. In the Qabalah it is called the Admirable or Wonderful Intelligence, the Supreme Crown, to show that 1 represents the determining, ruling, directive and volitional aspect of consciousness. This primary mode of consciousness is concealed behind all veils of name and form. It is the consciousness of the true Self or I AM—the Onlooker, seeing creation through countless eyes, manifesting itself through innumerable personalities. Ageless Wisdom teaches that all things are manifestations or projections in time and space of the powers of the I AM. In short, the I AM, or number 1, is the essence, substance, energy and consciousness expressed in all forms. Everything in the universe is the self-expression of the I AM. This is the first principle, the primary existence, the First Mover. In and through human personality it manifests as the waking *Self-consciousness.*

2. On the diagram this number begins at C, follows the upper circle through D to the center of the diagram, thence through the lower circle to E, and is completed by the horizontal line from E to F. The meanings of the number include:

Duplication, reflection, receptivity, dependence, alternation, antagonism, and the like. Qabalists call it Wisdom, the reflection of the perfect self-consciousness of the I AM. Wisdom is the mirror wherein the I AM sees itself. The number 2 is also named Illuminating Intelligence. It is that which illuminates the personal mind. It is the aspect of universal consciousness which manifests through human personality as grasp of the inner principles of the nature of the one Conscious Energy. In Hebrew occultism, 2 is also the particular number of the Life-force in all creatures.

3. The upper half of this figure is the same as the upper half of 2, from C through D to the center of the diagram. Its lower half begins at the center of the diagram, and follows the lower circle through F and B around to E. Among the meanings of 3 are:

Multiplication, development, growth, unfoldment, therefore expression. 3 signifies the actual outworking of the principles reflected from 1 by 2. In Qabalah, 3 is Understanding, looking forward into the field of manifestation, in contrast to Wisdom (2), which looks back to the self-knowledge of the I AM (1). Understanding is the concrete application of abstract Wisdom. Hence 3 is called the Sanctifying Intelligence, to convey the idea that through growth or expression comes the perfected manifestation of the potencies latent in the Limitless Light. On the form side, perfect realization (sanctification) requires perfected organism: in consciousness, it is perfected faculty and function.

4. This figure starts with the vertical line of the figure 1 (A to B on the diagram), and adds two other lines — A to G, and G to H. Thus drawn, 4 shows in its upper portion a triangle, symbol of the number 3, and in its lower portion a T-square, a geometrical symbol of 4 itself. Triangle and T-square are among the most important instruments of the draftsman. They have occult reference to the esoteric side of geometry. They suggest planning, surveying, topography and the like. From these considerations are derived the following meanings of 4:

Order, measurement, classification, recording, tabulation, and so on. Because of these meanings Qabalists make 4 the number of memory. Because the Life-power's perfect memory of its own potencies and of the needs of even the least of its centers of expression cannot be supposed to fail, the idea of Beneficence ("good-givingness") is also assigned to 4. This beneficence is not wasteful prodigality. All the gifts of the Life-power are measured out. Every center of expression receives exactly what is coming to it, always. Therefore the number 4 is called the Measuring Intelligence.

5. On the diagram, the first line of this figure is the horizontal, C to D. The second is vertical, C to I. The third includes five-sixths of the lower circle, from I through F and B to E. Meanings of 5 include:

Mediation (because 5 is the middle number between 1, Beginning, and 9, Completion), adaptation, means, agency, activity, process, and the like. 5 is the dynamic Law proceeding from abstract Order (4).

To primitive minds, the working of Law seems to be the operation of many forces, mostly hostile to man. Hence 5 is the number of versatility, and one of its names in Qabalah is Fear. Ignorant persons endeavor to propitiate the power they fear. Their sacrifices are the beginning of religious ritual. Hence 5 is the number of religion.

A better, though incomplete, knowledge of Law sees it as a relentless, harsh, mechanical expression of mathematical principles, taking no account of human needs and aspirations. This is the interpretation of the materialist, who sees the Law as a mighty power. Hebrew sages take account of this also, and say that 5 is the number of Strength and Severity, as well as of Fear.

Finally, to seers and sages, Law appears as the manifestation of perfect Justice, whereby man, whose numeral symbol is also 5, may so adapt natural conditions that he may realize progressive liberation from every kind of bondage.

5, then, is the number of versatility, because it shows

the changing aspects of the One Law, inspiring fear in the ignorant, perceived by the materialist as relentless strength, and understood by the wise as undeviating justice. This One Law is the root of all operations of the Life-power, and is therefore called Radical Intelligence. The root-consciousness expressed through human personality is this One Law of mediation or adaptation. Man can change conditions. This is the secret of his power to realize freedom.

6. On the diagram, this is a continuous line from D to A, down through the ellipse (on the Involution curve) to B, then around the lower circle to E. Its symmetry suggests the philosophical conception of Beauty. This is the direct outcome of ideas expressed by the preceding numerals.

A free Life-power (0), knowing itself perfectly (1), grasping all possibilities of what it is in itself (2), understanding just how these possibilities may be worked out into expression (3), never forgetting itself, or any detail of the perfect order of its self-manifestation (4), and developing that order through the agency of a perfectly just law or method (5), must inevitably be working toward a perfectly symmetrical, balanced, and therefore *beautiful*, result. This idea is implicit in the following meanings of 6:

Balance, equilibration, symmetry, beauty; harmony of opposites, reciprocity; complementary activities, polarity, love. It is named Intelligence of Mediating Influence or Intelligence of the Separated Emanations.

7. On the diagram, this is composed of two lines—the first horizontal, from C to D, the second diagonal, from D to E.

To exhaust the meanings of 7 would take as many pages as an encyclopaedia. It is the great Biblical number, many books in both the Old and the New Testaments being written on a plan of sevens—seven chapters, seven subdivisions, and so on. On this point, see the literary introductions in Moulton's *Modern Readers' Bible.* The more important occult meanings of 7 are:

Rest, safety, security, victory. To the ancients 7 represented temporary cessation, not final perfection, as some have thought. In Hebrew, the word for "seven" and that for "oath" are closely related, since the security and safety of a sworn compact were represented in Hebrew thought by 7.

This number stands for the logical consequence of the ideas symbolized by the numbers preceding it in the series. A perfect Life-power, working in the way outlined in the explanation of 6, cannot be supposed to fail. Omnipotence must ultimately, no matter what present appearances may be, arrive at a triumphantly successful conclusion to all its undertakings. The Great Work is as yet unfinished. The Cosmic Experiment has not come to completion, but when we consider the nature of the Source of that experiment, the nature of the Worker in that work, reason assures us that it must succeed, down to the minutest detail. The aspect of consciousness to which 7 corresponds is called the Occult or Hidden Intelligence.

8. On the diagram, this is a figure composed of the upper and lower circles within the ellipse. In writing it, we begin at A, describe a descending "S" to B, and return on an ascending inverted "S" to A. Thus the form of the figure suggests vibration by the shape of the lines, and alternation by the two kinds of motion used in describing it. It is also the only figure except 0 which may be written over and over again without lifting pen from paper. Thus in mathematics the figure 8, written horizontally, is the sign of infinity. Among its occult meanings are:

Rhythm, alternate cycles of involution and evolution, vibration, flux and reflux, and the like. It represents also the fact that opposite forms of expression (that is, all pairs of opposites) are effects of a single Cause. (See, on this point, Isaiah 45, verses 5 to 7).

This number 8 is the digit value of the name IHVH (Jehovah), 888 is the numeration of the name Jesus in Greek, and 8 is not only the "Dominical Number," or "Number of the Lord," in Christian numeral symbolism, but is also the particular number of the god called Thoth by Egyptians, Nebo by Assyrians, Hermes by Greeks, and Mercury by Romans. Thus 8 is preeminently the number of magic and of Hermetic Science. Its Hebrew name is Splendor, and the aspect of consciousness to which it corresponds is called Perfect Intelligence. The Hebrew adjective translated "perfect" is ShLM. A noun spelt with the same letters means "peace, security, health, wealth, satisfaction," and thus refers to the perfect realization of the success represented by the number 7.

9. On the diagram, it begins at D, follows the upper circle down to the center of the diagram, continues back to D, then along the line of the ellipse, on the right side of the diagram, to E. As last of the numeral symbols, 9 represents the following ideas:

Completion, attainment, fulfilment, the goal of endeavor, the end of a cycle of activity. Yet, because 8 indicates Rhythm as part of the creative process, completion is not absolute cessation. The end of one cycle is the beginning of another. This fact is the basis of all practical occultism. Nobody ever comes to the end of his tether. Nobody ever reaches a point where nothing more remains to be hoped for, where nothing remains to be accomplished. Every End is the seed of a fresh Beginning. In Qabalah, therefore, 9 is called Basis or Foundation, and corresponds to the mode of consciousness named Pure or Clear Intelligence, because the completion of any process is the pure, clear, unadulterated expression of the intention or idea which initiated that process.

10. Ten combines the ellipse of superconsciousness (0) with the vertical line of self-consciousness (1). It is the

number of perfection and dominion. Read from right to left, from units to tens (as all composite figures should be read symbolically), it suggests the outpouring of the limitless Life-power through the initiative, specialization and concentration of the I AM. Qabalists call the number 10 the Kingdom. The mode of consciousness assigned to it is the Resplendent Intelligence — brilliant, glowing, full of life and power. In one esoteric text this mode of intelligence is said to have its seat in Understanding, and Understanding is the number 3, or Sanctifying Intelligence. What is meant is, that in order to have the resplendent, glowing consciousness of mastery, one must have also, as a basis, the sanctifying, perfecting, organizing power of Understanding. Our citizenship in the Kingdom-of-Heaven-on-Earth is determined by the degree of our understanding.

Such is the outline of the ten primary numbers, according to Ageless Wisdom, as handed down to us through the Sages of Israel. It affords a basic clue to the meaning of Tarot.

For instance, the whole book, or pack of cards, contains 78 pages. Interpreting the number 78 from the foregoing, we see that it represents the expression of the Splendor of the Perfect Intelligence (8) through the Victory of Occult Intelligence (7). Precisely, this is the great purpose of Tarot.

In the practical work of the Builders of the Adytum, the esoteric meanings of the numeral symbols have been expanded into a series of eleven statements, or affirmations. These are entitled *The Pattern on the Trestleboard*, because, while they are at all times true of the real Self at the heart of every human personality, they are not intended to be taken as vainglorious claims to *personal* attainment. They will aid the reader to remember the main attributions of the numbers 0 to 10. More than this, they have, during the last twenty-five years, proved their value as seed-ideas which, planted in the mind by thoughtful and purposeful repetition, bear rich fruit in mental and spiritual unfoldment.

THE PATTERN ON THE TRESTLEBOARD

This is truth about the Self:

0. All the power that ever was or will be is here now.
1. I am a center of expression for the Primal Will-to-Good which eternally creates and sustains the universe.
2. Through me its unfailing Wisdom takes form in thought and word.
3. Filled with Understanding of its perfect law, I am guided, moment by moment, along the path of liberation.
4. From the exhaustless riches of its Limitless Substance, I draw all things needful, both spiritual and material.
5. I recognize the manifestation of the undeviating Justice in all the circumstances of my life.
6. In all things, great and small, I see the Beauty of the divine expression.
7. Living from that Will, supported by its unfailing Wisdom and Understanding, mine is the Victorious Life.
8. I look forward with confidence to the perfect realization of the Eternal Splendor of the Limitless Light.
9. In thought and word and deed, I rest my life, from day to day, upon the sure Foundation of Eternal Being.
10. The Kingdom of Spirit is embodied in my flesh.

III

CONSTRUCTION OF THE TAROT

THE TAROT is a book, disguised as a pack of cards. Fifty-six of its seventy-eight pages are called minor trumps. These are divided into four suits, distinguished by emblems like those on Spanish or Mexican playing-cards. The names of the suits are: Scepters or Wands; Cups; Swords; Coins or Pentacles. In the seventeenth century, French card-makers altered these, the original suit-emblems, to the Clubs, Hearts, Spades and Diamonds familiar to everybody.

Basically, the suits represent the four worlds, or planes, mentioned in Chapter I. The wands (clubs) correspond to the archetypal world, to the element of fire, and to I in IHVH. The cups (hearts) correspond to the creative world, to the element of water, and to the first H in IHVH. The swords (spades) correspond to the formative world, to the element of air, and to the V in IHVH. The coins or pentacles (diamonds) correspond to the material world, to the element of earth, and to the second H in IHVH.

In each suit are ten minor trumps, numbered consecutively from Ace to Ten. Thus the meaning of any numbered card in the minor trumps may be determined by combining the meanings of its number with the characteristics of the world represented by its suit. All the Twos, for example, suggest duplication, alternation and the like, and every one of them has some relation to the idea of Wisdom. So with the other numbered cards.

Besides the numbered cards, every suit of minor trumps contains four courtcards, instead of the three found in modern packs of playing-cards. They are:

16

KING, symbol of Spirit, the essential Self in man;

QUEEN, symbol of Soul, the inner "pattern" part of a particular human personality;

KNIGHT, symbol of that particular focus of energies, and of the personal sense of selfhood, which constitutes the Ego seated in the heart of a particular human personality;

PAGE, symbol of body, the personal vehicle of a particular human being.

The King of Wands is the idea of Spirit, the Queen of Wands the idea of Soul, the Knight of Wands the idea of personal energies, and the idea of what may be called "Egoity," the Page of Wands the idea of body. Similarly the courtcards of Cups symbolize the patterns of Spirit, Soul, personal energies and body; those of Swords stand for the processes requisite to the manifestation of Spirit, Soul, personal energies and body; those of Coins or Pentacles represent the actualized manifestation of Spirit, Soul, personal energies and body in a particular human being.

The more important part of the Tarot, with which this book is mainly concerned, consists of twenty-two cards, called major trumps. These are pictures, numbered consecutively from Zero to Twenty-one. Every major trump has a special title, which affords an important clue to its meaning. In addition, every major trump corresponds to one of the twenty-two letters of the Hebrew alphabet.

This alphabet differs from others in that every letter has a name. These twenty-two letter-names are Hebrew nouns, and every one of them designates some familiar natural object. They follow one another in logical sequence, bringing to the mind's eye a series of pictures. These pictures call up in every human mind, irrespective of race, certain basic associations of ideas. Hence, in studying any major trump of the Tarot, we begin with the mental image called up by the name of the Hebrew letter to which it corresponds.

In addition to the clues afforded by the numbers and titles of the major trumps, or Keys, and by the associations of ideas suggested by the letter-names, we find others derived from certain traditional occult interpretations of the Hebrew letters. These are given in an ancient volume of Qabalistic wisdom. The name of this book is the *Sepher Yetzirah*, or *Book of Formation*. From it are taken all occult attributions of the Hebrew alphabet given herein, with the exception of the attributions of the sun, moon and planets to the seven letters technically known as "doubles," because each of them has a hard and a soft pronunciation.

In all ancient copies of *The Book of Formation*, the planetary attributions to the double letters are purposely mixed, in order to mislead uninitiated readers into whose hands the book might fall. The correct attributions were reserved for mouth-to-ear instruction. When the first edition of this book was published in 1927, these attributions had never appeared in print outside the writings of the present author, except in one article published in *The Occult Review* for March, 1910, and in certain other publications more or less directly inspired by the author of that article. He received his knowledge from an occult society, under seals of secrecy which he violated by his publications of the true correspondences. He has been followed by other members of the same society, who offer the excuse that bad management in the society itself threatened the loss of its knowledge. Whether this be a valid excuse for breaking a solemn obligation, the reader must judge for himself; but it is only fair to add that the society in question rests under grave suspicion of having acted with considerably less than good faith in imposing obligations to keep secret knowledge which was by no means its exclusive possession, and to custody of which it had, to say the least, a most dubious title. The present writer worked out the attribution of the planets to the double letters from hints given in *The Book of Formation*, and from the Tarot itself, in the year 1907. His knowledge of the attributions was therefore in the nature of a recovery, and he violates no obligation in making it public.

Instead of tabulating all the letters and their meanings together, this book will give a separate explanation of every letter in connection with the major trump to which it corresponds. The various meanings and attributions should be read, digested and elaborated by every student who seeks to arrive at the deeper significance of Tarot.

In the first edition of my book, entitled *Introduction to the Study of the Tarot*, the descriptions of the symbolism were based on the Tarot known as the "Rider pack," drawn by Miss Pamela Coleman Smith under the supervision of Dr. Arthur Edward Waite. Dr. Waite had access to many occult manuscripts relating to Tarot. In some of his later writings he endeavored to throw dust in the eyes of the uninitiated by pretending to believe that the attribution of the cards to the letters exposed by the revelations before-mentioned was not the true arrangement. Yet his own rectifications of the symbolism and numbering of earlier exoteric versions of this picture book of Ageless Wisdom are sufficient evidence that he understood and accepted the validity of this attribution.

For example, in accordance with an old esoteric tradition, he transposed the numbering of the cards named Strength and Justice. Exoteric editions of Tarot, current in Italy and France subsequent to the eighteenth century, gave the number 11 to Strength, and 8 to Justice. In the Rider pack these numbers were reversed, as they are in Tarot packs belonging to certain occult schools.

The reason for this is that whatever card is numbered 8 represents the zodiacal sign Leo, and the picture entitled Strength shows a woman taming a red lion. Similarly, whatever card is number 11 corresponds to the sign Libra, and the picture entitled Justice shows a woman, carrying the scales (Libra). Furthermore, a great many details in the twenty-two major trumps of the Rider pack depend for their meaning on this same attribution of the major trumps to the Hebrew letters. These were pointed out in the first edition of *Introduction to the Study of the Tarot.*

In the present work, the twenty-two illustrations are reproductions of the Tarot Keys used by the Builders of the Adytum. They were drawn by Jessie Burns Parke, of Boston, under the supervision of the present writer. This was felt to be necessary for two reasons: 1. the obscuration of certain details in the symbolism, so that captious critics might find reason for doubting the interpretations; 2. the alteration of other Keys, so as to make them expressions of Dr. Waite's personal ideas, rather than correct statements of their original meaning.

The twelve flaming fruit on the tree behind the male figure in Key 6, The Lovers, is an example of the obscuration just mentioned. In the Rider pack it is by no means clear that every one of these is a triple flame. Another such detail is the substitution, in Key 14, of iris flowers for the rainbow which, in our version, as in the esoteric versions as yet unpublished, is placed over the head of the angel. To be sure, one who is sufficiently familiar with mythology might see a relation between the flowers and the rainbow goddess Iris; but there can be no question as to the meaning of the bow itself.

Keys 4, 13 and 19 of the Rider pack afford examples of marked departure from the traditional Tarot symbolism. This will be evident to anybody who has opportunity to compare the Rider Keys with the crude exoteric designs reproduced in Papus' book *The Tarot of the Bohemians*, or with those published in the same book after designs made by Oswald Wirth.

Miss Parke, unfortunately, adhered rather too closely to the tricks of style used by Miss Smith when the latter drew the Rider pack. In spite of this, she succeeded admirably in executing a set of Tarot Keys which are explicit in the details of their symbolism. There are no "blinds" in this version, and every symbol is intended to mean just what it is said to signify in the explanations given in the following chapters.

The attribution of the major trumps to the Hebrew alphabet is the crux in Tarot study. Eliphas Levi knew it, but could not give it, because he received it from a secret order. He did, however, announce the fact that the major trumps correspond to the Hebrew letters, and then proceeded to give an attribution so patently absurd that one wonders how it ever gained credence.

The absurdity consists in putting the picture numbered Zero between those numbered Twenty and Twenty-one. Yet even this affords a clue to the correct arrangement. Eliphas Levi evidently chose this position for the Zero Key because the latter was thereby assigned to the only Hebrew letter (besides the one to which it rightly belongs) which is a symbol of Spirit.

The letter Shin, next to the last in the Hebrew alphabet, has the value 300, and 300 is the numeration of the Hebrew words RVCh ALHIM, Ruach Elohim. The English of these words is *Life-Breath of the gods*, or *Spirit of God*. Hence Qabalists call Shin the "Holy Letter," because its number is the number of the name of the Divine Spirit. By assigning the Zero Key to this letter, Levi apprised his readers that the Tarot Fool is a symbol of the Holy Spirit.

There is, however, another letter in the alphabet which is also a symbol of Spirit, or Life-Breath, and this is Aleph, the first of the series. By attributing the Zero trump to Aleph we put it in its correct place, and then the other Tarot Keys are brought at once into correct relation to the letters whose occult meanings they symbolize.

It is, of course, obvious that in a series of numbered pictures including Zero and ending with Twenty-one, the logical place for Zero is at the beginning of the series. Zero is the mathematical symbol for the No-Thing which we are obliged to think of as subsisting before the manifestation of the relative Unity or Beginning represented by 1.

Again, there is a graceful allegory in the introduction to the *Zohar*, that classic of Qabalism, which tells how all the letters, beginning with Tav, and working backward through the alphabet, came before the Lord to prefer their claims to being accepted as the means whereby He would begin His creation. One by one they were rejected, until the letter Beth was chosen, because, being the initial letter of the Hebrew word signifying "Blessing," it was truly representative of the beneficent character of the whole creation. This same letter Beth is the first letter in the Hebrew text of Genesis.

Beth having been accepted, after the rejection of all the letters following it in the alphabetical series, there remained the letter Aleph. So the Lord promised Aleph that, as a reward for modesty, it should be forever the first of all the letters, and the special symbol of the Divine Spirit.

Here we have additional reason for the attribution of the Key numbered 1, that is, The Magician, to the letter which has 2 for its numeral value. The subsisting Spirit, self-sustained before the beginning of manifestation, is No-Thing or Zero. So also is the sound of the letter Aleph an unaspirated breath, or simple out-breathing. The letter Beth, on the contrary, is a true consonant, and, even in English, is the initial of the verb "begin." Aleph and Zero both symbolize the formless Spirit. Beth and One both stand for the first step in the series of creative activities.

Dr. Waite, Manly P. Hall, and some others have objected that this arrangement makes the numbers of the Keys and the numbers of the letters conflict. The answer to this is that the numbers printed on the Keys have one purpose, while those assigned to the letters have another.

The values of the Hebrew letters are used to determine the numerations of words. The numbers printed on the Tarot Keys determine the order of the pictures in the series. What is more, the letter-values of the Hebrew alphabet are not serial. From Aleph to Teth they are the digits from 1 through 9; from Yod to Tzaddi they are reckoned by tens, from 10 through 90, and from Qoph to Tav by hundreds, from 100 through 400.

Thus the same objection, were it at all valid, would

apply to Levi's attribution, which assigned Key 1 to Aleph, Key 2 to Beth, and so on. This seems plausible, on the surface, because the series of Keys from 1 to 9 then corresponds by number to the digit values of the letters from Aleph to Teth. Key 10, were this arrangement correct, would correspond also to Yod, which has 10 for its value. But Key 11 will then be assigned to a letter numbered 20, Key 13 to a letter numbered 40, and so on. Then, at the end of the series, Key 0 is assigned by Levi to a letter numbered 300, while Key 21 is attributed to a letter numbered 400.

Finally, if we use the arrangement given hereafter, the symbols on the pictures do agree, without question, to the occult meanings of the letters to which they are assigned. Those meanings do not have to be read into the pictures. Each symbol may be tested by comparison with the researches of the best authorities, from the most ancient writers down to the present. These are universal signs, and their fundamental significance is the same the world over, in all periods of history, in all forms of religion, in all varieties of philosophy. They are, in fact, drawn from that stock of images, common to all men everywhere, stored in what Dr. Carl Jung calls the "collective unconscious."

These pictorial images are those we weave into dreams. They are the symbols of poets, dramatists and novelists, as well as the substance of the visions of seers and prophets. Thinking in pictures is the fundamental activity of the human mind. We see before we say. Words are but labels for man's visual imagery.

Thus the letters of the Hebrew alphabet, because they are nouns, are actually twenty-two labels for mental pictures. From the same stock of pictures, by association, are drawn the occult attributions of the letters, and the symbols of the Tarot Keys. To make this clear, and to establish the correctness of this long-hidden attribution of the major trumps to the letters, is one of the main purposes of this book.

This attribution is as follows:

The Tarot

0. The Fool, Aleph.
1. The Magician, Beth.
2. The High Priestess, Gimel.
3. The Empress, Daleth.
4. The Emperor, Heh.
5. The Hierophant, Vav.
6. The Lovers, Zain.
7. The Chariot, Cheth.
8. Strength, Teth.
9. The Hermit, Yod.
10. The Wheel of Fortune, Kaph.
11. Justice, Lamed.
12. The Hanged Man, Mem.
13. Death, Nun.
14. Temperance, Samekh.
15. The Devil, Ayin.
16. The Tower, Peh.
17. The Star, Tzaddi.
18. The Moon, Qoph.
19. The Sun, Resh.
20. Judgment, Shin.
21. The World, Tav.

In connection with the following explanations, you will find it useful to arrange the major trumps on a table, in the following order:

```
                  0

     1   2   3   4   5   6   7

     8   9  10  11  12  13  14

    15  16  17  18  19  20  21
```

In this arrangement, the Zero Key is placed above the others to indicate that it precedes the whole series, and is not really included in the sequence of numbers. The pictures in the top row refer to powers or potencies; those in the middle row are symbols of laws or agencies; those in the bottom row represent conditions or effects. Thus Key 1 is the power which works through the agency symbolized by Key 8 to modify the conditions or effects typified by Key 15. Again, Key 2 stands for the potency or principle which operates through the agency symbolized by Key 9 to modify the conditions represented by Key 16. And so on, through the series.

Careful study of this tableau will reveal certain harmonies of number which are helpful in getting at the deeper meaning of the Keys. For example, the middle card in any horizontal row is the arithmetical mean term between three pairs of Keys on either side of it. That is, Key 4, in the top row, is the arithmetical mean between Keys 1 and 7, 2 and 6, and 3 and 5. Similarly, Key 11, in the middle row, is the mean between Keys 8 and 14, 9 and 13, 10 and 12. On the bottom row, Key 18 is the arithmetical mean between Keys 15 and 21, 16 and 20, and 17 and 19.

In like manner, every Key in the middle row is the arithmetical mean between the Key above it in the tableau, and the Key below. Thus 8 is the mean between 1 and 15, 9 the mean between 2 and 16, and so on.

In this tableau, therefore, Key 11 stands as the mean between ten pairs of Keys. These are, 1 and 21, 2 and 20, 3 and 19, 4 and 18, 5 and 17, 6 and 16, 7 and 15, 8 and 14, 9 and 13, and 10 and 12. The members of these ten pairs stand in diametrically opposed positions in the tableau, and Key 11 is at the center of the whole scheme, where it is obviously a symbol of the agency which effects balance, or equilibration, among all the forces symbolized by the other Keys.

Careful inspection of the twenty-two Keys, laid out in this tableau, will reveal many other interesting and enlightening correspondences. It will also make clear the principle of antithesis utilized in designing the Keys. This principle may be observed also by comparing the letter-names of the Hebrew alphabet. It is applied consistently throughout the series, and conforms to fundamental laws of human thought.

For instance, in the top row of Keys, a male figure, the Magician, stands outdoors, in a garden. In Key 2, the central figure is a virgin priestess, sitting inside a temple. Key 3, by contrast to the virgin High Priestess, is a pregnant woman, sitting in a garden. Key 4 is her consort, clad in armor, sitting on a height, with the river that waters his wife's garden far below. Key 5 contrasts the power of the church, designated in the exoteric title as the Pope, with the power of the State symbolized by the Emperor. Key 6 is, in contrast to Key 5, an outdoor scene, suggesting the untutored innocence of Adam and Eve in the garden. Key 7 has in the background a city, and all the rest of the symbolism is made up of details having to do with a relatively advanced stage of civilization. Bear this principle of antithesis in mind. As applied to Tarot, it means that any Tarot Key is in direct contrast to the one which immediately precedes it in the series.

To what, then is Key 0 a contrast? To what else but Key 21, the last card? For the very word Tarot is an artificial word, made up of the letters of the Latin noun, *Rota*, written round a circle, as, indeed, you may see by inspecting Key 10. Start at the bottom of the wheel, with R, and go round the wheel, clockwise, and the four letters spell ROTA. Begin at the top, and follow round the wheel in the same direction, and the four letters spell TARO. Go on from 0 to your starting-point, and you come to T again, and so spell out TAROT.

The Tarot, then, is a symbolic wheel of human life. We might, indeed, arrange these twenty-two pictures in a circle, with the Keys equally spaced, like figures on a clockface. Then, when we had gone round the circle from 0 to 21, we should, in completing the circuit, arrive at 0 again. This is an important clue to some of the deeper meanings of Tarot. Ponder it well, and from within you will come more light than we could shed in page after page of explanation.

The Fool

0 **THE FOOL**

IV

KEY 0: THE FOOL (ALEPH)

Aleph is the Hebrew equivalent for the English A. Its numeral value is 1. In Roman characters used for transliterating Hebrew words throughout this book, its name is ALP, meaning Bull or Ox.

This is believed by many to establish the time of the invention of the alphabet as being during the astronomical period called the Taurean Age, when the bull was the god-symbol dominant in the leading religions of the world. Apis in Egypt, Mithra among the Persians, Dionysos among the Greeks, all had the bull or ox as a symbol.

Since oxen pulled the plow and threshed the grain in primitive husbandry, besides pulling the carts which carried the farmer's produce to market, they became the symbols for the motive power in agriculture. Agriculture is the basic form of civilization, thus the ox represents the power at work in all forms of human adaptation and modification of natural conditions. Oxen, again, are symbols of wealth, as our own English adjective, *pecuniary*, derived from the Latin *pecus:* cattle, clearly shows. Finally, oxen and bulls, the world over, represent creative energy, life-power, the vital principle of plants, animals and men, which comes to us in physical form as the light and heat of the sun.

The Hebrew name for this vital principle is *Ruach* (RVCh). Its literal, basic meaning is "Breath." It is equivalent to English *Spirit*, Latin *Spiritus*, Greek *Pneuma*, and Sanskrit *Prana*. All these words mean air or breath. They all designate the all-pervading cosmic energy which animates every living creature. This Ruach is specifically attributed to the letter Aleph in the Qabalistic *Book of Formation*.

29

Fiery or Scintillating Intelligence is the mode of consciousness assigned to Aleph. Breath keeps a fire alight in our bodies. In both Old and New Testaments we are told: "The Lord our God is a consuming fire." To define the primal mode of the Life-power—the first aspect of the cosmic vital principle—is impossible. Yet wise men have ever agreed that it is like fire, and the most recent discoveries of modern physics demonstrate the fact that the "something" whereof all things are made is a radiant, fiery energy. Occultism adds the thought that this energy is the working power of pure consciousness, which plays upon that energy, is inseparable from it, and directs all its manifestations *from within*. This idea of inherent directing consciousness, combined with current scientific explanations of the electro-magnetic constitution of matter, gives precisely the conception which Qabalists convey by the term Scintillating Intelligence.

In the color-scale used by some Western schools of occult science, the element of air and the fiery Life-Breath are represented by a clear, pale shade of yellow. Since the discovery of the planet Uranus, the higher octave of Mercury, this planet has been attributed to Aleph, and is represented by the pale yellow tint just mentioned. Its tone vibration is E-natural. The planetary name Uranus, it should be noted, is the English adaptation of a Greek word meaning "sky."

Furthermore, those who believe, with the present writer, that all language, and, in consequence, all accepted scientific nomenclature, is an evolutionary process having its origin in the Universal Mind, may reach the conclusion that the noun *uranium*, derived from Uranus, is by no means a chance designation for the chemical element whence are derived the thought-designed and man-made elements, neptunium and plutonium, those terrible "sky-powers" which appear, at present, to threaten the extermination of humanity in a frenzy of insane suicide. Yet these same powers might, if rightly applied, so change our globe that it would become a veritable Paradise. Ageless Wisdom, in spite of all appearances to the contrary, holds fast to the conviction that the Directing Intelligence will so work itself out in human thought that new, constructive uses for the "sky-power," going far beyond what most of us can now imagine, will bring to fulfilment the ancient promise of a new heaven and a new earth, peopled by regenerated humanity.

The Zero Key elaborates the occult meanings of *Aleph*. Its number identifies it with the No-Thing whence all things proceed. The Qabalists called this Limitless Light. In connection with *Aleph*, we find this Light represented as the active principle of existence, prior to actual manifestation. The picture of the Fool, therefore, does not show this principle as it really is, because the Absolute transcends finite comprehension. Yet the symbols show it as it has revealed itself, in a measure, to the wise.

The Fool is pictured as a youth, because we are obliged to think of the Absolute in terms of our own experience. To our minds the Life-Breath presents itself in human form; but behind this personal seeming sages discern something higher, typified in the picture by the white sun. This higher something is an impersonal power, manifesting as the limitless energy radiated to the planets of world-systems without number, streaming to them from their respective suns.

In manifestation, this energy is temporarily limited by living organisms. Of these, the primary class is the vegetable kingdom, represented by the green wreath which binds the Fool's fair hair. The hair itself is yellow, symbolizing the radiant energy of the Life-Breath. The higher class of organisms is the animal kingdom, evolved from the vegetable world, and represented here by the red feather rising from the wreath. This feather is also a symbol of aspiration and of truth. The colors of wreath and feather, green and red, are complementary, as are the kingdoms they symbolize.

The cosmic Life-Breath is forever young, forever in the morning of its power, forever on the verge of the abyss of manifestation. It is neither male nor female, hence this gay young traveler's figure might be either a lad, or a girl disguised, like Rosalind. Actually it is the Heavenly Androgyne.

Always it faces unknown possibilities of self-expression, transcending any height it may have reached at a given time. On this account the sun behind the traveler is at an angle of forty-five degrees in the eastern heaven, as Swedenborg says the celestial sun remains forever in the spiritual world. The spiritual sun never reaches the zenith, for from the zenith it would have to descend, and the idea here intended is that infinite energy never can reach a point in manifestation whence it must begin to decrease in power. On this account, too, the Fool faces North-West, toward a direction which, for Masonic and other occult reasons, has for milleniums been symbolic of the unknown, and of the state just prior to the initiation of a creative process.

The traveler's eager gaze is fixed rapturously on a distant height, beyond and above him. He is That which was, and is, and shall be — the deathless, fadeless life-principle, subsisting eternally behind all modes of existence.

His inner robe is dazzling white, representing the light of perfect wisdom. Dimly traced, in the folds at the neck of this white garment are the Hebrew characters of the Divine Name, IHVH, Jehovah. This name, according to Qabalists, is represented by the three parts of the Hebrew character for the letter *Aleph*.

The white undergarment is almost wholly concealed by the black coat of ignorance, lined with the red of passion, fire, and material force. This outer garment is embroidered with what seems to be a floral decoration, but the unit of design, repeated ten times, is a yellow wheel, containing eight red spokes. Around this wheel are seven green trefoils.

The yellow color of the wheel represents air or breath. The eight red spokes combine the number 8, symbol of rhythm, with the color red, and refer to the rhythmic action of the fiery activity which sets the Life-Breath into whirling, wheeling motion. The seven trefoils are green, color of organic life in the vegetable kingdom, and particular color of the planet Venus in color-symbolism. Each trefoil represents one of the "Seven Spirits of God," and one of the seven great "rays" of the universal creative energy. They are trefoils because every one of these seven force-rays has a triple expression: (a) integrating, (b) equilibrating, (c) disintegrating.

There are ten repetitions of this unit of design, to refer to the ancient doctrine that all manifestation is in ten aspects or phases—"ten ineffable numerations, ten and not nine, ten and not eleven," as *The Book of Formation* says. In one of these wheels, near the bottom of the Fool's coat, is placed the Hebrew character for the letter Shin. This refers to the connection between the letters Aleph and Shin, which are both alphabetical symbols of the fiery Life-Breath, or Holy Spirit.

In addition to these ten wheels, there is on the right breast of the Fool a yellow circle enclosing a triple flame of red. This represents the state of the Life-Breath prior to manifestation, when the universal energy (yellow disk), although it has the triple potency of expression (the triple flame) within itself, has not yet organized that potency into the rhythmic, whirling motion which is the basis of all modes of expression.

On the Fool's left shoulder is a golden eight-pointed star. Close to it is a silver lunar crescent. These are the Sun and Moon, or gold and silver, of the alchemists. They refer also to Surya, the hot, electric, solar current of Prana described in books on Yoga, and to Rayi, the cool, magnetic, lunar current of the same Prana. Fundamentally, these are two modes of the One Life-Breath. Their activity is both universal and personal. In humanity they are active in the nerve currents of the physical body.

The black wand over the Fool's right shoulder is a measuring tool. It supports a wallet, having a flap sewn with ten stitches. The lock of this flap is in the form of an eye. On the wallet, below the flap, is a picture of an eagle.

The wand is a symbol of will, of which attention, the wand itself, is the essence, and to which memory, the wallet, is closely linked. The wallet contains the summed-up experience of previous manifestations, because, at the beginning of every new cycle of self-expression, the Life-power carries with it the essence of all its experiences in former cycles.

The lock of this wallet is in the form of an eye, which stands for the All-seeing Eye of Freemasonry, and for the Eye of Horus, in Egyptian symbolism. It suggests, also, that through the development of a higher type of vision we may gain access to the treasure of stored-up experience in the universal memory. The ten stitches on the flap have the same meaning as the ten wheels on the Fool's coat, and refer to the ten types of vision, or higher perception, developed by occult practice.

The eagle on the wallet refers to the zodiacal sign Scorpio. Thus it intimates that the wand and wallet together may be understood to be phallic emblems, referring to the natural process whereby the accumulated experience of the Life-power is passed on from cycle to cycle, through an endless chain of living organisms. In occultism, moreover, the awakening of the higher vision symbolized by the eye on the flap of the wallet is brought about by practices which redirect and sublimate the bodily forces related astrologically to the sign Scorpio.

The rose in the Fool's left hand is white, to indicate freedom from the lower forms of desire and passion, and also to show that it refers to the spiritual prototype of desire. It is a cultivated flower, showing (as do other details of the Fool's vesture and equipment) that he has come from a previous scene of cultural activity, from a plain somewhere behind him on his journey. For, as corresponding to Aleph, the Fool symbolizes cultural activities. At the waist, the robe is encircled by a girdle having twelve circular ornaments, of which seven are visible. It refers to the twelve signs of the zodiac, through which are expressed the powers of the seven heavenly bodies known to the ancients. Thus the girdle typifies Time, and since the belt must be removed in order to take off the black coat, here is a plain intimation that to rid ourselves of ignorance and passion we must overcome the illusion of Time, which is, as Kant long ago proved, purely a creation of the human intellect. A practical occultist learns to replace Time by Eternity, and practices daily to accustom himself to leading the *timeless* life.

The citrine or olive of the Fool's hose (the tint varies in various versions of Tarot) refers to the element of earth, and to the tenth numeration, or aspect of the Life-power, which Qabalists call the Kingdom. His yellow shoes refer to the element of air, which is the vehicle of the Life-power.

The icy peaks in the distance show that the cold, abstract principles of mathematics are above and behind all the warm, colorful, vital activities of cosmic manifestation.

The little white dog is a descendant of wolves and jackals. Thus he is a human adaptation, whereby something given in a wild and dangerous state by the unmodified processes of nature has been changed into a friend, helper and companion of man. He also indicates the truth that all subhuman forms of the Life-power are elevated and improved by the advance of human consciousness. Finally, for symbolic reasons going back to ancient Egypt, he is a symbol of intellect, subordinate to superconsciousness.

The Fool, then, symbolizes what Dr. Waite, in his *Key to the Tarot*, calls "the state of the first emanation." He is the primary aspect of universal consciousness, which we term superconsciousness. He is the cosmic Life-Breath, about to descend into the abyss of manifestation.

Because he symbolizes the state of the Life-power just prior to the beginning of a cycle of self-expression, he also represents inexperience. For until the Life-power actually enters into the particular activities of such a cycle, it can have no real experience of those activities. It is because of this inexperience that the subtle wise men who invented Tarot called this Key "The Fool."

Another reason was that they were familiar with the philosophic truth that superconsciousness is above reason, imagination, thought, feeling, and all other states of self-consciousness. *The Mystical Theology of Dionysius* therefore says of God: "He has neither imagination nor reason, nor does He know anything as it is, nor does anything know Him as He is."

Apply these words to a man, and you call him a fool. Furthermore, the attempt to limit Divine Consciousness to personality, making God a big man, is mentally to create a foolish divinity. Finally, the title of the Zero Key refers to that "foolishness of God which is wiser than men." This means that although superconsciousness has no actual experience of those facts and events which are the warp and woof of human knowledge, its inherent awareness of the principles of its own nature far transcends the limits of human wisdom.

THE MAGICIAN

1 | THE MAGICIAN | ב

V

KEY 1: THE MAGICIAN (BETH)

Beth (B, value 2) means "house." The first thing about a house is its location, determined by survey, an application of geometry. In its building, architecture, geometry, adaptation of materials, and many other practical applications of science are involved. Time was when the whole art of building was called a "mystery," and was under the direction of the priests of Thoth-Nebo-Hermes-Mercury. House-building is part of Hermetic science, and survivals of this idea are preserved in the rituals of Freemasonry.

Mercury is the astrological attribution to Beth. It represents both the planet and the "god." Understand by "god" an aspect of universal consciousness, personified. The "gods" are the Elohim of the Hebrew scriptures, wherein it is written of man, "I said, Ye are gods."

To Mercury or Hermes (Hiram) the Egyptians attributed their forty-two books of science, embracing astronomy, astrology, arithmetic, geometry, medicine, grammar, logic, rhetoric, music, magic, and so on. Mercury or Hermes was the great magician and transformer, bearing the caduceus, or wand of miracles, which survives to this day as a symbol of the healing art. He was, nevertheless, only the messenger of a divinity higher than himself— merely the transmitter, not the originator, the channel rather than the source.

Astrologically, the Mercury vibration represents intellect. In the color-scale used throughout these lessons it is yellow, the color assigned to Spirit and air, but a deeper tint than that assigned to Uranus. The musical tone is the same, E-natural.

Beth is one of the seven double letters, so called because they have in Hebrew both a hard and a soft pronunciation.

To every double letter is assigned a pair of opposites. To Beth and Mercury, because the letter and planet designate an aspect of consciousness which destroys as easily as it creates, the pair assigned is *Life and Death.*

Intelligence of Transparency is the mode of consciousness. "Transparency" means "letting light shine through." Here we have the same idea of transmission that is suggested by Hermes as the transmitter of the messages of the higher divinity. Clearly the mode of consciousness called transparent must be one which affords a free channel of communication, which permits the free passage downward and outward of the superconscious Light which is above and within.

Above is the direction assigned to Beth, because the mode of consciousness corresponding to the letter is the superior term of human personal consciousness. As Hermes was herald of the gods, directing the soul (according to Egyptian mythology) through the mysteries of the underworld, or nightside of nature, so is this superior phase of human personal consciousness the initiator, and the conductor of human personality through the mazes of life. It is the number ONE consciousness, the Ego-consciousness, the "I am I," which is sometimes called "objective mind"; but, because it is first of all consciousness of the indwelling presence of the superconscious Self, we prefer to term it self-consciousness. It is the Onlooker, the director, the superior personal mode of universal Conscious Energy. It is your everyday waking consciousness.

The Magician is the correct title of Key 1, used in all versions of Tarot belonging to occult fraternities, though it is sometimes debased into *The Juggler* in exoteric packs. Magic is simply the ancient name for science, particularly for Hermetic science.

The true magic presides over house-building because it shows us how to erect actual houses so as to take advantage of occult properties of the earth-currents of magnetic vibration. The higher phases of magic, moreover, have to do with the building of the "house" of personality, with the rearing of the Temple of Spirit, the "house not made with hands, eternal in the heavens."

The Magic of Light presides over life and death because it has to do with laws and principles whereby self-conscious states of mind initiate and determine subconscious reactions. These reactions make for life or for death, according to the patterns which self-consciousness formulates and passes down to the subconscious plane.

Every true magician knows that all his practice has a mathematical, geometrical basis. By the aid of occult geometry he has traced nature to her concealed recesses. He uses geometrical formulae and diagrams in his practical work.

Finally, though he knows himself to be above nature, he understands that his operations succeed to the degree that his thought, word and action transmit faithfully the powers of the plane above him. The greatest magicians know themselves to be no more than channels for the Life-power, clear window-panes through which the light of wisdom within the house of personality streams forth into the objective world.

The arbor of roses over the Magician's head corresponds to the letter-name, Beth, because an arbor is the simplest type of shelter. Red roses, symbols of Venus, represent the desire-nature. Here they suggest that the power which the Magician draws from above is modified or qualified by desire. This is true of all self-conscious activity. Every moment of our waking consciousness is motivated and conditioned by some type of desire.

The horizontal figure 8 over the Magician's head is the ancient occult number ascribed to Hermes. (See explanation of the number 8 in Chapter 2.) This horizontal 8 is also a symbol of the Holy Spirit. It means dominion on the horizontal plane; that is, dominion in material affairs, because one of the oldest symbols of matter is the horizontal line.

In contrast to the Fool's yellow locks, the black hair of the Magician signifies ignorance. Yet this ignorance is limited by knowledge, for a white crown encircles the Magus' brow. It passes round his forehead at the location of the brain areas particularly active in self-conscious mentation.

His uplifted right hand suggests power drawn from above. The wand it holds aloft is a double-ended phallic symbol. It is phallic, because the nerve-force used to maintain the reproductive functions may be purified and sublimated by certain magical procedures. The purification is suggested by the whiteness of the wand. Its two points, exactly alike in form, remind us of the Hermetic axiom, "That which is below is as that which is above, and that which is above is as that which is below, for the performance of the miracles of the One Thing." They also indicate subtly that the lower manifestations of the force here symbolized are not destroyed nor atrophied in the process of purification and sublimation. Finally, the two points refer to the duality of all magical operations, which are of two great classes—those leading to the higher expression of life, and those resulting in death.

The Magician's down-pointing left hand symbolizes direction of power to a plane below. It makes the gesture of concentration. The pointing finger is that attributed to the planet Jupiter. From this finger, palmists judge the degree of a client's powers of leadership and direction. It is the executive and determinative finger. The gesture plainly conveys the notion that concentration is the secret of the direction and control of forces below the plane of self-conscious awareness.

Of the double gesture made by the Magician's hands Dr. Waite says: "This dual sign is known in very high grades of the Instituted Mysteries. It shows the descent of grace, virtue and light, drawn from things above and derived to things below. The suggestion throughout is therefore the possession and communication of the Powers and Gifts of the Spirit."

The Magician's white inner robe has the same significance as the white garment of the Fool. The serpent girdle signifies wisdom (serpent) and eternity (biting his tail). Dr. Waite says, "Here it indicates more especially the eternity of attainment in the spirit." The serpent is colored blue-green, because it is also a symbol of the serpent-force which is utilized in all magical practice. This force is related to the sign Scorpio, which, in our color-scale, is associated with blue-green.

The Magician's red outer garment represents desire, passion and activity. Its color is that of the planet Mars, which astrology associates with action and initiative. This red robe has no binding girdle. It may be slipped on or off, at the Magician's pleasure. This means that self-consciousness may enter into action, or abstain from it, according to circumstances. Thus this bit of symbolism is connected with the power of choice, or of selection, characteristic of self-consciousness.

The table before the Magician represents the "field of attention" in modern psychology. The word "table" has also affinities in language with the word "measurement," inasmuch as to classify and arrange is to *tabulate*. Note that the corners of the table had to be squared, and that the cylindrical legs, which have capitals like Ionic columns, required the use of compasses, and, by their capitals, suggest the "orders" of architecture.

"On the table in front of the Magician," writes Dr. Waite, "are the implements of the four Tarot suits, signifying the elements of natural life, which lie like counters before the adept, and he adapts them as he wills." As elements of natural life they refer to fire (wand), water (cup), air (sword) and earth (coin or pentacle). They symbolize also the four worlds, and correspond to the letters of IHVH.

The Magician's problem is to arrange them in proper order. In ceremonial magic, these implements are the staff, the cup of libations and divination, the magic sword, and the pentacle or talisman. On the pentacle are written or engraved words, numbers, geometrical figures, and sigils. These are determined by the nature of the magical operation to be effected by the powers they represent. In this instance, the sigil on the pentacle is the pentalpha, the five-pointed star, or Pentagram. Of this sign Eliphas Levi says:

"The Pentagram expresses the mind's domination over the elements, and it is by this sign that we bind the demons of the air, the spirits of fire, the spectres of water, and the ghosts of earth. It is the star of the Magi, the burning star of the Gnostic schools, the sign of intellectual omnipotence and autocracy. It is the symbol of the Word made Flesh...The sign of the Pentagram is called also the sign of the Microcosm. Its complete comprehension is the key of the two worlds—it is absolute natural philosophy and natural science."

From the foregoing quotation you may come to understand the nature of the work to which the Magician in Tarot is directing his powers. Be careful not to take the first sentence of the quotation too literally. There is a meaning behind the surface meaning. Find it yourself.

In practical, every-day life, the implements of the Magician are the four life-essentials: light (wand), water (cup), air (sword) and food (pentacle). The combination of these life-essentials in proper order and proportions is the task of every practical occultist.

Finally, the four implements correspond to four ancient esoteric admonitions, which sum up the whole practical application of occult law. These admonitions are: (1) TO WILL (wand); (2) TO KNOW (cup); (3) TO DARE (sword); (4) TO BE SILENT (pentacle). The last, in some respects, is the most important. "Occult" means "hidden," and one of the first duties of a practical occultist is the practice of silence.

The Magician's garden is the antithesis to the barren height whereon stands the Fool. The garden is fertile and productive. It is itself a symbol of the subconscious plane of mental activity. From this teeming soil come forth the productions which give shape and form to the ideas of the Magician. He is shown as a gardener, like Adam, of whom an old legend says that he was put into the Garden of Eden to grow roses.

Like Adam, self-consciousness is the namer of objects. Like Adam, personal self-consciousness is formed by the power of the "Lord," who is That which was, is and shall be. Like Adam, the personal self-consciousness is formed of the "dust of the ground," because self-consciousness is an aggregate of myriads of tiny sense-impressions (dust) originating in that cosmic operation of the Life-power which makes the environment of personality, and is the true ground or basis of all self-conscious experience.

"Beneath," writes Dr. Waite, "are roses and lilies, the *flos campi* and *lilium convallium*, changed into garden flowers, to show the culture of aspiration." Red roses typify Venus and the desire-nature. White lilies represent abstract thought, untinged by desire. The roses are developed from the five-petalled wild rose, and thus they symbolize the number 5, which has for its geometrical correspondence the Pentagram. As symbols of desire, they represent that phase of subconscious response to self-conscious direction which has to do with art, invention, and the adaptation of the principles of abstract truth to practical ends. Because all desires are related to sensation, there are five roses, corresponding to the conventional five senses.

Lilies have six petals, and in cross-section their flowers show the Hexagram, or six-pointed star, which is the symbol of the Macrocosm. Pure science concerns itself with the study of the powers of the Macrocosm, and with the laws of those powers. Because these laws and forces operate in the four worlds or planes mentioned in Chapter 1, the number of lilies shown in the picture is four.

Thus all meanings of the letter Beth, the number 1, and

the symbols of the Magician refer to powers of the self-conscious phase of personal mental activity. These powers are directed primarily to the control of forces and things below the self-conscious level. The energy utilized comes from above, from superconsciousness. It is fixed and modified by acts of attention. Concentration is the great secret of the magical art. True concentration is perfect transparency, in which personality becomes a free, unobstructed channel for the passage downward and outward of the superconscious radiant energy. Herein is the secret of true volition, and Eliphas Levi tells us, "All magic is in the will."

The
High Priestess

2   HIGH PRIESTESS

VI

KEY 2: THE HIGH PRIESTESS (Gimel)

Gimel, third letter of the Hebrew alphabet, is a double letter. Its name means "camel." Because camels are used for transportation, for carrying goods from one place to another, the letter-name suggests travel, communication, commerce, and like ideas. Because merchants and pilgrims use camels in making journeys together, Gimel suggests association, combination, coexistence, partnership, and the like. Because a camel has means for carrying extra supplies of water, it symbolizes moisture. Finally, the camel is the "ship of the desert," and its humps look something like a crescent.

Gimel is represented in English by the letter "G," which has also a hard and a soft pronunciation. Hard as in "girl." Soft as in "geranium." The numeral value of Gimel in Hebrew arithmetic, and in reckoning the numeration of Hebrew words, is 3.

The Moon is the celestial body assigned to Gimel. First, because the Moon is a satellite, *accompanying* the earth. Second, because the Moon waxes and wanes, just as a caravan is first seen as a tiny dust-cloud on the rim of the desert, then grows larger and larger until it stops awhile at some oasis city, and then grows smaller and smaller as it journeys thence, on its way to its next destination. Third, because the lunar crescent resembles the shape of a camel's humps, also because, as the camel is the "ship of the desert," so is the Moon the "ship of the skies." Finally, the astrological nature of the Moon is cold and moist. The moon is the astrological symbol of personality, and of the memories carried from one incarnation to another by the subconscious mind. In our color-scale, the tint assigned to the Moon is blue, corresponding to the musical tone G-sharp, or A-flat.

As a double letter, Gimel designates the pair of opposites, *Peace and Strife*. For, as in the world peace and war are mainly dictated by the conditions of commerce, communication and transportation, so, in human personality, adjustment or maladjustment are largely determined by the response of subconsciousness to the things and people with whom we are brought into communication.

Uniting Intelligence is the mode of consciousness attributed to Gimel. As transportation (camel and caravan) brings distant places nearer together, and establishes communication between them, so does subconsciousness, which is the connecting medium between human personalities, unite us to one another—regardless of distance. Subconsciousness is the agency of telepathic communication.

Below is the direction attributed to Gimel. That which is below is secondary, subordinate, dependent, under control, subject to command, obedient. All these ideas are clearly related to the idea of "camel," as an obedient beast of burden. They relate in consciousness to the subordinate element of personal subconsciousness, at all times amenable to control by suggestions which originate in the mental activities symbolized in Tarot by the Magician, who represents self-consciousness.

The title, *High Priestess*, means literally "chief feminine elder," or primary receptive aspect of the Life-power. In Hindu philosophy this is *Prakriti*, the precosmic root-substance which is the substratum beneath all the objective planes of existence. Thus the woman in Key 2 is in one sense identical with the First Mother, or First Matter, of the alchemists, who often call this *Prima Materia* their Virgin Diana.

Diana is the goddess of the crescent Moon. She is also the Great Hecate of Greek occult philosophy. Hecate, often confused in ancient mythology with Luna, was supposed to have all secret powers of nature at her command.

In fact, the High Priestess corresponds to all the virgin goddesses of the ancient world — to Artemis, guardian and helper of childbirth, to Maia, mother of Hermes, to Bona Dea, who "out of modesty never left her bower, or let herself be seen of men," and to Kybele, whose sanctuaries were caves. Dr. Waite says "she is the spiritual Bride and Mother, the daughter of the stars . . . the Queen of the borrowed light, but this is the light of all." Thus she also represents Eve, before her union with Adam.

Her number, 2, has been explained heretofore. As a symbol of duplication, reflection, copying, transcription, reproduction, and so on, it relates definitely to memory, the basic function of subconsciousness. The number 2 also suggests the ideas of duplicity, deception, untruth, illusion, error and delusion. This is correct, because subconsciousness repeats and elaborates the mistaken results of faulty, superficial self-conscious observation. Being at all times uncritically amenable to suggestion, and at the same time the channel of telepathic communication, subconsciousness is the source of most of the foolish notions which cause our maladjustments. Something of this lies behind the Biblical allegory that Eve was the means of Adam's temptation and fall.

In contrast to the Magician, who stands upright in a garden, the High Priestess is seated within the precincts of a temple. The walls of the building are blue, and so are the vestments of this virgin priestess. Blue, the color assigned to the Moon, and to the element of water, represents the primary root-substance, the cosmic mind-stuff, which is the element particularly attributed to the Creative World. The High Priestess herself is a symbol of this root-substance.

The two pillars between which she sits are those of Solomon and of Hermes. Opposite in color, but alike in form, they represent affirmation (white pillar, bearing the letter Yod, initial of the word Jachin) and negation (black pillar, bearing the letter Beth, initial of the word Boaz). For strength (Boaz) is rooted in resistance or inertia, which is the negation of the activity which is the establishing principle (Jachin) of all things. The High Priestess sits between the pillars, because she is the equilibrating power between the "Yes" and the "No," the initiative and the resistance, the light and the darkness.

Alike in form, close to each other, opposite in color, the pillars represent three laws of the association of ideas and of memory. We associate things similar, things near together in space or time, things sharply contrasted.

The bases of the pillars are cubes. Thus they repeat the symbolism of the High Priestess' seat, which is a cubic stone. This will be explained in a subsequent paragraph. The capitals of the pillars, borrowed from Egyptian architecture, are in the form of lotus buds. They are buds, not opened flowers. In this detail they differ from the capitals in the Rider version of the High Priestess, but follow the design of the as yet unpublished esoteric Tarot. The reason the capitals are buds is that the High Priestess, as a symbol of virginity, is, in some measure, a type of latent, or undeveloped, powers. In the state of subconsciousness here symbolized, the forces of subconsciousness have not come to full bloom.

The veil between the pillars hints that the High Priestess is *virgo intacta*. It is a phallic symbol of virginity, but is embroidered with palms (male) and pomegranates (female), as if to suggest the union of positive and negative forces. Subconsciousness is only potentially reproductive, in the aspect represented by Key 2. It is, so to say, covered by a veil. Only when this veil is rent or penetrated by concentrated impulses originating at the self-conscious level may the creative activities of subconsciousness be released and actualized. Compare the arrangement of the palms and pomegranates on the veil with the diagram of the Tree of Life at the end of the book, and you will see that the position of the High Priestess corresponds to the path of Gimel, descending from Kether, the Crown, at the top of the diagram, to Tiphareth, Beauty, at the center. Note also that the number of Tiphareth, 6, corresponds to the six sides of the cube whereon the High Priestess sits.

The High Priestess wears a silver crown, reminding us that silver is the metal of the Moon. This crown shows the crescents of the waxing and waning Moon, with her full orb between. It is the horned diadem of the Egyptian Isis, another of the feminine deities personifying the root-matter of all things.

She sits on a cubic stone, a symbol of salt, which crystallizes in perfect cubes, and a reminder of the saltness of that mystical sea which is associated with the Virgin Mary. Since the time of Pythagoras, moreover, it has been taught openly that the cube is the regular solid representing "earth" or actual, material manifestation.

Thus the High Priestess sits on a cube because the basis of all subconscious mental activity is what has actually occurred, what actually exists. This underlying Reality is what is designated in Hebrew by the name IHVH (Jehovah), and to this word the figures required to define the proportions of a cube have special reference. Every cube has 6 sides, 8 points or corners, and 12 edges or boundary lines. The numbers required to express a cube's peculiar limitations being 6, 8 and 12, their sum is 26, and this is the sum of the values of the Hebrew letters Yod-Heh-Vav-Heh, or IHVH. What actually exists, what really is, what materialists and idealists alike misunderstand and misinterpret, is the real presence of That which was, is and shall be. This real presence is the basis of all subconscious activity.

The High Priestess wears a blue-white robe, suggesting coldness and moisture, which are the astrological properties of the Moon, and the characteristics of the element of water. The folds of this robe show a shimmering radiance, like that of moonlight on water, and, below the white pillar, this garment seems to flow out of the picture, like a stream. It symbolizes the "stream of consciousness" familiar to students of psychology. In Tarot, the robe of the High Priestess is the source of the river and of the pools which appear in several subsequent major trumps.

The scroll in the woman's lap is that of memory. In some versions of this Key it is a book, half-open. This is the record of past events, of all mental and physical states, indelibly impressed in subconsciousness. Subconsciousness is both universal and personal. Thus the memory record includes the past events of race-history, the past events of the history of the planet, and the past events of this whole cycle of cosmic manifestation. Hence the scroll is inscribed with the word "TORA," which is the phonetic equivalent of the Hebrew "Torah," or "Law." Yet this word is also related to the Latin ROTA, from which, as explained in Chapter 3, the very name TAROT is derived. Natural law is the cosmic subconscious record of every event in the innumerable cycles and sub-cycles of the Life-power's self-expression.

In the Rider pack, there is a yellow crescent at the feet of the High Priestess. This is good lunar symbolism, but it confuses the symbolic issues. This will be better understood after you have read the explanation of the Empress, in the next chapter.

The solar cross of equal arms on the High Priestess' breast shows the union of positive (upright) and negative (horizontal), male and female, active and passive, originating and duplicating elements. It also foreshadows the completion of the entire cycle represented by the twenty-two Tarot Keys, because this cross of equal arms is the original form of the Hebrew letter Tav, the final letter of the Hebrew alphabet. Again, this same cross stands for Hecate, who, among other things, was patroness of all cross-roads, according to Greek mythology. Finally, the arms of the cross are related to the number 4, or square of 2, as are the square sides of the cube.

THE EMPRESS

3   **THE EMPRESS**   **ך**

VII

KEY 3: THE EMPRESS (DALETH)

Daleth (D, value 4) originally signified the leaf of a door—
that which admits or bars; but it also symbolizes that
through which something passes. On this account some
writers say Daleth represents the womb, as the door of life.

The door itself, then, suggests defense, protection,
preservation, safe-keeping, conservation, and related
ideas. This is a clue to the mode of consciousness represented by Daleth. We shall find that this mode of consciousness has to do with personal safety, with self-
preservation, with defense against trouble and disease,
and with the storage, conservation and development of all
that is useful to us.

The idea of passage suggested by the doorway brings to
mind both ingress and egress, motion into and motion out
from. It also suggests transmission, diffusion, dissemina-
tion, separation (as when one thinks of a door as the
means of leaving a house), and so division, apportion-
ment, partition, administration. All these ideas are
definitely connected with the mode of consciousness
represented by Daleth.

Observe, also, how the principle of antithesis already
mentioned applies to the sequence of Hebrew letters, as
well as to the Tarot Keys. Aleph is a soft, open breathing,
barely vocalized, and the letter-name is associated with
the nomadic life of herdsmen, following their cattle
wherever pasturage is good. By contrast, Beth, the house,
implies a certain definiteness and fixity of location, and
the sound of "B" is a sharply vocalized consonant, expel-
ling the breath through the pursed lips. Gimel, the third
letter of the alphabet, is guttural in its hard pronunciation,
and dental in its soft utterance. The camel, moreover, is in

57

contrast to Beth, the house, because of the ideas of commerce, travel and communication with distant places. Now, when we consider Daleth, the door, we are brought back to the house again, so that the letter has in it somewhat of the root-significance of Beth. Yet it also partakes in a measure of ideas suggested by Gimel, since both departure and return are suggested by a doorway.

Venus is the planetary attribution to Daleth. She corresponds to the cow-headed Egyptian goddess Hathor (whose name, in some old Latin manuscripts, is occasionally spelled ATOR). Venus presides over child-birth, is a mother-goddess, and patroness of love, beauty and art. Astrologers say Venus rules the sense of touch, and has much influence on the disposition, especially on the desire-nature. In our color-scale, Venus is green, corresponding to the tone F-sharp or G-flat.

Wisdom and Folly are assigned by Qabalists to Daleth. The mode of consciousness assigned to Daleth is subconsciousness, and subconscious response to self-conscious interpretation and suggestion determines whether our ideas (mental offspring) are wise or foolish. The occult meanings of Daleth indicate clearly that this letter corresponds to subconsciousness. The latter has no power of inductive reasoning, but its power of deduction is practically perfect.

Now, the very word "deduction" means "leading away from," and deductive reasoning is separative, because it splits up an original premise into an indefinite number of particular consequences or applications. Whether the conclusions so reached shall be wise or foolish depends entirely on the soundness of the initial premise. The latter is formulated by self-conscious observation and inductive reasoning. If the premise be accurate and profound, the subconscious subdivisions and elaborations of the initial seed-thought will be on the side of wisdom. If the premise be inexact and superficial, the subconscious developments will be on the side of folly.

East, the direction assigned to Daleth, is the doorway through which the sun enters the world at the beginning of a day. It is the place of the birth of light. Similarly, subconsciousness is the womb of those ideas which enlighten the world. In Hebrew, the noun for East is AVR (pronounced "our"), and the word for Light has the same spelling, and practically the same pronunciation.

Luminous Intelligence, the Qabalistic name for the phase of consciousness represented by Daleth, requires little explanation. Subconsciousness enlightens us by its deductions from our observations and from our inductive reasoning. These deductions are not only illuminating, but they also make for our safety, self-preservation, and general welfare. Again, they enable us to share in the administration of our environment, assure us of our just portion of all good things, and enable us to find a way out of the limitations and bondage which imprison the unenlightened in cages built by their own ignorance and misunderstanding.

Key 3's title, *The Empress,* means literally, "She who sets in order." She is the feminine ruling power. She is also the consort of the Emperor, whose picture adorns Key 4 of the Tarot series. Her name contrasts with the High Priestess, which indicates the cold virginity of a cloistered devotee of the gods. In like manner, mythology contrasts the warm mother-goddess, Venus, with Diana, virgin-goddess of the Moon.

The scene harks back to some of the symbolism of Key 1, for it is a rich, fertile garden. In the background are cypress trees, sacred to Venus. Ripening wheat in the foreground is sacred to Isis-Hathor, as well as to Ceres, another mother-goddess. For this picture, primarily representing Venus or Hathor, corresponds also to other representations of Mother Nature.

The stream and pool in the background represent the stream of consciousness. Their source is the flowing robe of the High Priestess. The symbol of water falling into a pool is also a subtle intimation of the union of male and female modes of cosmic energy. For the stream is modified and directed by the Magician, and the pool represents the accumulation of influences descending from the self-conscious level. This stream waters the garden, and makes it fertile.

The Empress is a matronly figure, about to become a mother. Her yellow hair is bound by a green wreath of myrtle. Like the hair of the Fool, hers symbolizes radiant energy, and her wreath has the same general meaning as that around the head of the Fool. Myrtle, moreover, is a plant sacred to Venus.

The idea here conveyed is that the growth and organization of the plant-world is the work of cosmic energy operating at subconscious levels. Thus people who know how to reach the subconsciousness in plants can do almost anything with them. Luther Burbank's work was an outstanding example. What is more, growing plants respond to curses and to blessings, and those who succeed best in growing flowers are lovers of the plants they care for.

Like the woman in the Apocalypse (Revelation 12:1), the Empress wears a crown of twelve stars, and has a crescent moon under her feet. The stars are six-pointed, or hexagrams, to show that she has dominion over the laws of the Macrocosm, or great world. This crown of twelve stars, like the Fool's girdle, also symbolizes the zodiac, the year, and time. The silver lunar crescent under the Empress' feet indicates the fact that the subconscious activities she symbolizes have their basis in the primary powers of subconsciousness which Tarot pictures in the High Priestess. Actually, there is no fundamental difference between the latter and the Empress; but the High Priestess symbolizes the virgin state of the cosmic subconsciousness, as it is in itself, whereas the Empress typifies the productive, generating activities of the same subconsciousness, after it has been impregnated by seed-ideas originating at the self-conscious level represented by the Magician.

Besides the cypress trees, the myrtle and the wheat-ears, the seven pearls round the Empress' neck are Venusian. So is the green color of her robe. (In the Rider pack, the robe is white, ornamented with a floral design in which the units are astrological symbols of Venus.) Again, she bears a heart-shaped shield, on which is displayed a dove, sacred to Venus, and symbol also of the Holy Spirit. (The Rider pack shows a shield emblazoned with the conventional astrological symbol of Venus, and the circular part of the symbol is the Venusian green.) This heart-shaped shield is of copper, the metal of Venus. "Heart" in practical occultism means subconsciousness.

According to Dr. Waite, "the sceptre which she bears is surmounted by the globe of this world." Thus it implies dominance over the conditions of the physical plane. In our version, she carries the scepter in her left hand, and the globe is surmounted by a cross, so that the ornament on the head of the scepter is actually an inverted Venus symbol.

Psychologically, the Empress represents subconsciousness as the mother of ideas, the generatrix of mental images. The power by which she works is the power of subdividing seed-ideas, derived from self-consciousness. This is the power of deductive reasoning. The apparent multiplication of images is really the splitting-up of the seed-ideas into manifold presentations. This is symbolized by the multiplication of the original seed in the wheat-ears at her feet.

She is called the Empress because subconsciousness has control over all sequences of development in the material world. Occult science declares that this control extends even to the mineral kingdom, so that adepts in the direction of subconsciousness by suggestion are able to effect transformations even in the inorganic world, by purely mental means. The particular mental function peculiar to subconsciousness is imagination, based on memory.

THE EMPEROR

4 | THE EMPEROR | 7

VIII

KEY 4: THE EMPEROR (HEH)

Heh (H as in "honor," or E, value 5) is pronounced "hay." It means "window," (literally, wind-door). A window admits light (knowledge) and air (Life-breath, spirit) into the house (Beth) of personality. It also permits outlook, survey, supervision, control, and so on. Architecturally, windows are derived from doors. Furthermore, since they permit a survey of persons approaching a house, they enable the inhabitants of the house to decide whether to open the door to admit friends, or to bar it against enemies. The most important thing about a window is transparency, and this takes us back to the mode of consciousness attributed to the Magician.

Sight is the sense function attributed by Qabalists to the letter Heh. Vision, inspection, reconnaissance, watchfulness, care, vigilance, examination, calculation, analysis, induction, inquiry, investigation, and the like, are all associated in language. All depend largely on the sense of sight. Thus we may expect to find the mode of consciousness associated with this letter one which is active in this kind of mental operation.

Constituting Intelligence is the name given it in the Hebrew wisdom, and it is said to "constitute creation in the darkness of the world." To constitute is to make anything what it is, to frame, to compose. Constitution is closely related to authorship. The author of anything is its producer, originator, inventor, founder, begetter, generator, architect and builder. Authorship is therefore closely connected in our thought with paternity, and paternal authority depends on the fact that the father is head and founder of the family.

In this connection, it is interesting to find that the letter

Heh is employed in Hebrew precisely as we use the English definite article "the." The Constituting Intelligence is the defining consciousness.

This shows us, first of all, that the Constituting Intelligence must be a variant of self-conscious mental activity, because to define anything is to name it, and we have already associated self-consciousness with Adam, the namer. Definition, moreover, limits, sets boundaries, circumscribes. It specializes, particularizes, enters into detail, makes distinctions.

The qualities thus indicated are precisely those which enter into the making of a constitution for any form of society, and that constitution is the basic law and supreme authority for its particular social organization. Thus the letter Heh, as the definite article, implies regulation, order, law, and all related ideas. Laws are definitions, and it should always be borne in mind that what we call "laws of nature" are simply definitions or descriptions of a sequence of events in some particular field of human observation.

What is even more important for the occultist and the psychologist is that our personal definitions of the meaning of our experiences constitute suggestions which are accepted, without reservation, by our subconsciousness. Thus, in a sense, every man makes his own law, writes the constitution of his own personal world, and finds that his life-experience is the reproduction of that constitution through the working of subconscious responses.

Heh is the first of the twelve "simple" letters of the Hebrew alphabet, so called because each has but a single pronunciation. To it is attributed the first sign of the zodiac, Aries, the Ram.

Aries is a fiery, cardinal sign. It governs the head and face. It is ruled by Mars, significant of force, strength, energy, courage and activity. Mars rules iron, steel, surgery, chemistry and military affairs.

In Aries the Sun is exalted, or raised to its highest level

of power. The Sun has to do with health and vitality. It is the significator of high office, and of positions of rank and title, so that it represents rulership and authority. It also stands for the Ego, or individuality, in one's natal horoscope. Its metal is gold.

Aries is a scientific and philosophical sign, and this agrees with what has been said concerning the Constituting Intelligence, inasmuch as both science and philosophy have accurate definition as their basis. Astrologers say Aries represents rulership, government, guidance and leadership. The color corresponding to Aries is scarlet. The musical tone is C-natural.

North-East is the direction attributed to Heh. These directions are given in *The Book of Formation*, and have to do with a very important esoteric teaching, in which the manifested universe is represented as a cube, shown in occult diagrams with its western and southern faces visible to the observer. (See the accompanying illustration.)

The six faces of this cube and its interior center are assigned to the seven double letters of the alphabet. The three interior co-ordinates correspond to the three mother letters. The twelve boundary lines represent the twelve simple letters.

Thus, of the letters already considered, Aleph corresponds to the line extending inside the cube from the center of the upper face to the center of the bottom face, so that it is representative of pure Spirit (superconsciousness) as the link between the superior and inferior manifestations of the Life-power.

The letter Beth, corresponding to the direction Above, is assigned to the upper face of the cube. Gimel, corresponding to the direction Below, is assigned to the lower face. Daleth, corresponding to the direction East, is the rear face of the cube shown in the accompanying diagram. The letter Heh, which we are now considering, is assigned to the vertical edge of the cube, which is the point of junction between the eastern and northern faces, connecting the north-

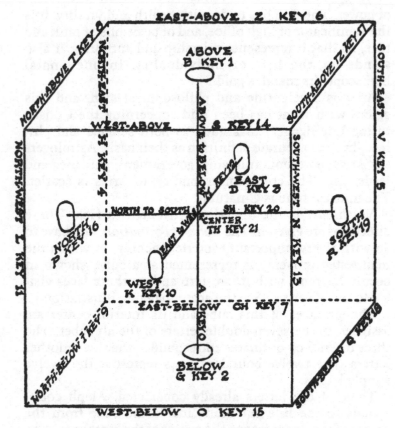

THE CUBE OF SPACE

east upper corner with the north-east lower corner.

No more than hints of this cube symbolism can be given in this introductory text, but we have thought best to include the figure of the Cube of Space, since careful study will reveal to discerning readers many clues to a deeper understanding of the Tarot symbolism.

In Tarot, the direction North, through the letter Peh, corresponds to Key 16, analyzed in Chapter 20, and East is, as we have said, represented in Tarot by Key 3, The Empress. Later on it will be evident that the Constituting

Intelligence combines the imagination and generation of ideas associated with the Empress with the destruction of structures of error, symbolized in Tarot by the lightning-struck Tower. Accurate definition requires clear imagery (Empress), and its application in action is always destructive to error (Tower). Note, furthermore, that the direction North is associated with Mars, the ruler of Aries, and that the direction East is associated with Venus.

The title of Key 4, *The Emperor,* means "he who sets in order," and from what has been said, it will be seen to be peculiarly applicable to this picture. It implies both authority and paternity. It also represents the head of government, the source of war, the war-making power, and so on. These ideas are related to the sign Aries, and to Mars and the Sun. They are ideas, moreover, which are in close correspondence to the meanings of the number 4 given in Chapter 2.

The orange background in the upper part of the picture refers to the exaltation of the Sun in Aries, because orange is the color of Key 19, The Sun, whose metal is gold. Below it are red mountains, of igneous rock. Both in form and color, these refer to the fiery quality of Aries. Red is also the color of this sign, and of Mars, its ruler.

These mountains in the distance are forbidding heights, in sharp contrast to the valley where the Empress sits. Barren, they represent vividly the sterility of mere supervision and regulation, unless there be something vitally warm and fruitful to set in order. On the other hand, it is the erosion of these barren rocks which provides the soil for the Empress' garden.

Far below, at the base of the mountains, flows a river. This is the same stream of consciousness that begins in the robe of the High Priestess, and waters the Empress' garden.

On the Emperor's shoulder is a ram's head, and another is shown on the southern face of the cube whereon he sits. Thus this second ram's head, combined with the face of the cube corresponding to South and to the Sun, suggests the exaltation of the Sun in Aries. Another intimation that this Key represents Aries is the astrological symbol of this sign, shown as an ornament at the top of the Emperor's helmet-like crown.

The monarch sits on a cubic stone, like that which is the seat of the High Priestess. This indicates that the mode of consciousness here symbolized has its seat or basis in laws of cosmic manifestation which are at work in the mineral kingdom. A very few laws suffice for all the complex manifestations of the Life-power, and they are operative on "low" planes as well as on "high."

The metal parts of the Emperor's helmet-like crown are of gold, a further reference to the exaltation of the Sun in Aries. The shape of the crown suggests the conventional helmet of Mars, ruler of Aries. Underneath the crown is a red cap, the color of which refers both to Mars and Aries.

The composition of the Emperor's figure deserves special mention. It is so drawn that the right hand, the left elbow, and the top of the head form the points of an equilateral triangle, while the legs suggest a cross. Thus the basis of the composition is an equilateral triangle surmounting a cross. This is the alchemical symbol for the fiery alchemical principle, Sulphur, closely akin to the Rajas or Agni Tattva of yoga philosophy, and therefore related to the element of fire, predominant in the sign Aries.

The Emperor is clad in steel armor. This further emphasizes his correspondence to the martial sign Aries, because iron and steel are the metals of Mars.

The ornamental flaps of his garment are purple. This is the color of royalty. It has reference also to the planet Jupiter, represented in Tarot by the Wheel of Fortune, because there is an occult relationship between 4, the number of the Emperor, and 10, the number of the Wheel of Fortune. We shall recur to this when we come to Key 10.

The yellow or gold scepter in the Emperor's right hand is a modified Venus symbol, another reference to the exaltation of the Sun in Aries. This scepter is also one form of the Egyptian *ankh*, or sign of life. It means that the power of regulation is chiefly derived from the exaltation of solar energy in the sense of sight, and in the mental vision which is the inner correspondence thereto.

The globe in the monarch's left hand is the conventional symbol of dominion. It is red, color of Mars, and on it is an inverted, gold T-square. The square is a symbol of the use of mathematics and geometry and planning. Because it is shaped like a letter "T," it is in correspondence with Tav, the last letter of the Hebrew alphabet, to which the planet Saturn is assigned. What this hints is that the order and dominion exercised by the Emperor bring about an inversion or reversal of the Saturnine power of limitation. Right definition is itself a sort of limitation, which sets us free from slavery to circumstances because it enables us, through right knowledge, to establish new boundaries, to enlarge our horizon.

The Emperor is an old man, with a white beard, shown in profile. This is one marked divergence from the Rider pack, which shows him full-face. Dr. Waite registers his opinion that nothing particular signifies from showing the Emperor in profile. Yet none of the old exoteric packs of Tarot show him full-face, nor does the unpublished esoteric version. The more recondite reasons for preferring the profile which shows only the left eye of the monarch have deep roots in Qabalistic philosophy and symbolism, but they go far beyond the scope of the present volume. Enough to say that the present writer has been instructed in this Qabalistic tradition, and thinks it of sufficient importance to retain the older symbolism. For that matter, Dr. Waite had the same occult instruction, and must have known that Key 4's place on the Qabalistic Tree of Life, through its connection with the letter Heh, makes the use of the profile symbolism, by which Qabalists invariably represented the Ancient of Days, practically imperative for any representation of the Emperor.

The Emperor is obviously the consort of the Empress. He is, in fact, essentially identical with the Magician, after the latter's union with the High Priestess has transformed her into the Empress, and has made him the father of her children.

It is on this account that the Emperor follows the Empress in the series. As the Magician he is only potentially a father, just as the High Priestess is only a potential mother. After his consort has borne him children, the Emperor has opportunity for actual exercise of his parental authority.

In one sense the Emperor represents the Grand Architect of the Universe, the Ancient of Days. He is the supreme NOUS, or Reason, the constituting power, alike of the great world and of the little, of the universe and of man.

Psychologically, therefore, he represents the self-consciousness of man, when its activities are engaged in the work of inductive reasoning whereby errors arising from superficial interpretation of experience are overthrown. He is the definer, the lawgiver, the regulator. He is the ruling mental activity in human personality. He frames the constitution of your personal world.

The
Hierophant

5   **HIEROPHANT**   ו

IX

KEY 5: THE HIEROPHANT (Vav)

Vav (V, U, W, value 6) means "nail" or "hook"; something
to join the parts of a building together, therefore
associative, like Gimel, also something to support hanging objects, therefore something on which other things
depend. A nail is a fastening, a link, a means of union. As a
means of support, it is linked in thought and language
with such ideas as aid, assistance, sustenance, furtherance
and ministry. It will be seen presently that these ideas are
not only directly connected with the occult meanings of
Vav, but also with the symbolism of the Hierophant.

In Hebrew, the letter Vav is the equivalent of the English
"and." Thus the grammatical use of the letter is derived
directly from its literal meaning. The conjunction "and"
links together a series of nouns describing various objects,
as, "apples *and* pears *and* lemons." It also introduces
dependent clauses in a sentence. In Hebrew, the letter Vav
is used in precisely the same way. Thus, like a nail, it binds
the parts of a sentence together, and clauses or phrases
introduced by it hang from it, like pictures supported by
hooks driven into a wall.

Now, the central thought here is "union," and this is the
exact English translation of the Sanskrit noun "yoga." The
same Sanskrit noun is the root of our word "yoke," and
some authorities are of the opinion that the original hiero-
glyphic symbol for Vav was a picture of a yoke such as is
used for harnessing oxen.

Yoga is a system of practice whereby the personal consciousness is linked to the universal conscious energy. Its
object is direct, first-hand experience of those phases of
reality which are the basis of all religions. The founders of
religions are persons who have such experiences, and the

contention of practical occultists is that this kind of experience may be repeated whenever the right conditions are provided. It is not a capricious gift from on high. It is not miraculous. Rare it may be, but it is perfectly natural, and a human being who addresses himself earnestly to preparing himself for this kind of experience will find what he seeks. We shall find, presently, that the Hierophant in Tarot is a symbol of the mode of conscious activity which takes form in such experiences.

Hearing, which unites man to man by speech, and man to God by the Word of the Inner Voice, is the sense attributed to Vav. Jesus said often, "He that hath ears to hear, let him hear." This is a technical formula of Ageless Wisdom.

It refers to the development of the interior sense of hearing just mentioned. In Sanskrit, the noun *sruti*, literally "hearing," is the term for revelation. "It alone can remove that nescience which is innate in human nature," says one ancient book. Similarly, the prophets of Israel declare, again and again, "Thus saith the Lord," as if they were reporting things heard. Two of them, Samuel and Elijah, were directly aware of the Divine Presence as a Voice.

What was true then is true now. Knowledge of the higher aspects of reality comes to us through the soundless sound of an Inner Voice, which often speaks as plainly as any voice heard with the physical ear. The reason is that the hearing centers in the brain are stimulated by higher rates of vibration, which serve as means of communication between ourselves and more advanced thinkers. Many persons have flashes of this experience, and our recognition that this is so is expressed by the oft-repeated statement, "Something seemed to say to me."

Triumphant and Eternal Intelligence is the name of the mode of consciousness corresponding to Vav. It is "triumphant" because it gives assurance of the ultimate victory of the Life-power over all apparent obstacles now seeming to stand in the way of the completion of the Great Work. It is "eternal" because it not only carries with it a positive conviction of immortality, lifting personal consciousness out of the limitations of Time into the realization of the freedom of Eternity; but also because the revelations of the Inner Voice enable us to solve particular problems by applying principles which, as soon as we perceive them, we recognize as being true, yesterday, today, and forever.

Taurus, the Bull, a fixed, earthy sign, is attributed to Vav. It is ruled by the planet Venus (Key 3, The Empress), and is the sign of the exaltation of the Moon (Key 2, The High Priestess). The name of the sign itself shows a secret correspondence with the higher spiritual things, and with superconsciousness, inasmuch as Aleph, the Bull, is the letter corresponding to Ruach, the Life-Breath, pictured in Tarot by the Fool. The Voice of the Hierophant gives verbal form to the vision of the Fool. Revelation (Key 5) is the communication of the transcendent knowledge of superconsciousness, in so far as that knowledge can be put into words.

Astrologically, too, the sign Taurus is representative of latent powers and energies, of secretiveness and reserve — ideas clearly suggested by the title and symbolism of the Hierophant. Furthermore, Taurus rules the neck, which is the link between head and body; and in the neck is located a psychic center dominated by the Venus vibration. The exaltation of the Moon in Taurus indicates that the powers of subconsciousness, especially the powers of memory and of recollection, have their highest manifestation in the mental activities pictured by Key 5. In our color-scale, Taurus is red-orange. Its musical tone is C-sharp or D-flat.

South-East, the direction attributed to Vav, is represented on the Cube of Space by the vertical line connecting the lower south-east corner with the upper south-east corner. This edge of the cube is also the line along which the southern and eastern faces of the cube are conjoined. In Tarot, South is related to Key 19, The Sun, and East is related to Key 3, The Empress. Here is suggested a blending of solar and Venusian qualities. The Sun is a great center of what Hindus call Prana. The Venusian vibration is that which manifests in mental imagery. Occultly, the blending of these two vibrations is the mingling of the universal Conscious Energy with the imaginative, generative powers of subconsciousness. In the activity symbolized by the Hierophant, these two phases of the Life-power are combined.

Hierophant means "revealer of sacred things." It was the name of the chief officer in the Eleusinian Mysteries, and signifies that which makes known the hidden import of the appearances whereby we are surrounded. In many versions of Tarot this Key is named "The Pope," but Dr. Waite rightly says that this is "a particular application of the more general office that he symbolizes."

On the other hand, "Pope" really means "Father," and when we consider the relation of Key 5 to the Qabalistic Tree of Life, we notice that the path of Vav is the one which begins in Wisdom, the second Sephirah, and descends to Mercy, the fourth Sephirah. (See diagram of the Tree, at the end of this book.) Thus, since the Sephirah Wisdom is also known as Ab, the Father, it becomes evident that the Hierophant, as an expression of that Sephirah's outflowing energy, is not altogether misnamed when it is called "The Pope."

We do not agree with Dr. Waite that the Hierophant "is the ruling power of external religion, . . . exoteric orthodox doctrine, . . . the outer side of the life which leads to the doctrine." On the contrary, he is the *pontifex*, the "bridge-maker" who provides a connecting link between outer experience and interior illumination.

He sits on a throne, between two stone pillars. These, and the throne, together with the background, are gray, a color associated with Wisdom, because gray is the tint resulting from equal mixture of any two complementary colors. Since color complements are also opposites, gray stands for the perfect balance of all pairs of opposites, and this is the practical aspect of Wisdom, the second

Sephirah. Thus the gray background of Key 5 affords a very definite clue to the position of this Key on the Tree of Life, since, in colored representations of the Tree, the second Sephirah is painted gray.

The design on the capitals of the pillars is a phallic symbol of union. The pillars themselves repeat the motif of duality, and suggest the laws of association represented by the pillars of the High Priestess.

The throne is also of stone, and the word "stone" has a very special meaning in the Bible and in the Qabalah. In Hebrew, "stone" is ABN, *ehben*. The first two letters of this word, Aleph and Beth, are the letters of the noun *Ab*, meaning "Father," and this is one of the Qabalistic names for the second Sephirah. The last two letters, Beth and Nun, spell the word *Ben*, meaning "Son," and this is the Qabalistic name for the sixth Sephirah, Beauty, which, as you can see from the diagram of the Tree, is the central point, and, so to say, pivot, of that diagram. Thus in the word ABN, *ehben*, as Qabalists say, "the names of the Father and the Son, of Wisdom and Beauty, are conjoined"; and this is the main reason for the many symbolic uses of the word "stone" throughout the Scriptures.

At the back of the throne, on either side of the Hierophant's head, are two horned circles, representing the sign Taurus. The same Taurus symbol is shown also on the throne behind the Hierophant in the Rider pack, but it is drawn in such a way that few persons unacquainted with the occult meanings of Vav would be likely to notice it. This partial concealment may have been due to the fact that Dr. Waite seems to have been somewhat concerned lest he should expose the deeper occult significance of Tarot to any but initiated students.

The crown is a triple tiara, like the Pope's crown. It is of gold, symbolizing radiant energy and wisdom. It is ornamented with three rows of trefoils: top row, 3; middle row, 5; bottom row, 7. (In the Rider pack, the middle row has 7, and the bottom row has 5.) The total number is 15, the numeral value of the Hebrew divine name IH, Jah. This name is that associated by Qabalists with the second Sephirah, and affords another clue to the attribution of Key 5 to the path joining the second Sephirah to the fourth.

Since any trefoil represents the number 3, fifteen of them stand for 3 x 15, or 45, number of the name ADM, Adam. Here is a reference to the Qabalistic doctrine that man or Adam is God's image of Himself — that the primary thought in the Mind of God, prior to all manifestation, must be God's awareness of His own nature and powers, and that this awareness is the true "image of God," designated by the name Adam.

The three trefoils in the upper row designate the threefold nature of the Life-power. The five in the second row represent the five modes of manifestation — the Quintessence and the four elements, or the five Tattvas of Hindu philosophy, which are the subtle principles of sensation. The seven in the bottom row correspond to the Seven Spirits of God, to the seven sacred planets, to the seven alchemical metals, and to the seven chakras, or interior "stars," of the yoga schools. Here we have, also, the *three* principles of the alchemists, their *five* modes of the manifestation of the One Thing, and their *seven* so-called "metals."

In the Rider pack, the tiara is surmounted by a black "W," indicating the correspondence of Key 5 to the letter Vav. In the B.O.T.A. (Builders of the Adytum) version, the ornament at the top of the crown is a small sphere, symbolizing the archetypal world. Below it, the three rows of trefoils, in descending order, symbolize the creative, formative and material worlds.

The outer robe of the Hierophant is red-orange, the color corresponding to Taurus. It has for trimming a border of blue-green, complementary to red-orange, and corresponding to the sign Scorpio, the sign opposite and complementary to Taurus. At the neck, this outer garment is caught with a clasp in the form of a silver crescent. This is a symbol of the Moon, which is exalted in Taurus. Its position at the Hierophant's throat is a reminder that Taurus rules that part of the human body.

Under this red-orange robe the Hierophant wears a garment of blue, like that of the High Priestess, and having the same meaning. Under this is a white garment, like that of the Fool, and having the same significance. The crosses on the Hierophant's white shoes refer to the union of male and female, positive and negative forces, and to the order (4, cross) which results from that union. Similar crosses are shown on the backs of his hands, on the carpet under his feet, and on the handles of the crossed keys. These ten crosses repeat the symbolism of the ten circular ornaments on the outer garment of the Fool.

Hanging from the crown, behind the ears of the Hierophant, is an ornament in the form of a yoke. This refers to the primitive meaning of the letter Vav. It falls behind the Hierophant's ears to call attention to these organs of hearing.

In his left hand, the Hierophant holds a yellow or golden staff. It symbolizes the dominion of the Life-power through the planes of nature, represented by the knob at the top, with three cross-bars below it. These latter correspond in meaning to the three rows of trefoils on the tiara, and the knob at the top of the staff corresponds to the circular ornament at the top of the crown. The scepter is yellow or golden, to show that the power exerted in the Hierophant's dominion is the power of the universal radiant energy.

The crossed keys at the Hierophant's feet are the familiar symbols of the power of the Papacy. Yet they have a deeper meaning. One is silver, the other golden. They stand for the solar and lunar currents of radiant energy, which, as nerve-currents in the human body, are utilized as keys to open the inner doors leading to higher modes of awareness.

The golden key is the key of heaven, wherein the Sun is ruler. The silver key is associated with hell because of the correspondence between the Moon and Hecate, whom the Greeks worshiped as a deity of the underworld. Thus the silver key relates to the powers of subconsciousness, and the golden key represents the powers of superconsciousness.

The square dais suggests the number 4, symbol of order and measurement, as if to suggest that however far beyond our present experience the higher consciousness may go, it rests on a solid basis of fact and reason. The dais is covered with a red-orange carpet, corresponding by this color to Taurus. The four circles on it enclose crosses—the Venus symbol folded in upon itself. They represent the manifestation of IHVH in the four worlds. Black and white checker-work at the edges of the carpet remind us of the Masonic mosaic pavement, which represents the alternation of light and darkness in the manifestation of the Life-power.

The priests kneeling before the Hierophant wear robes which repeat the motif of the flowers in the Magician's garden. Their robes are ornamented with yellow palliums, symbols of the yoke, or union. These are yellow, because the yoke is that of Mercury, or intellectual perception. The priest who wears lilies personifies thought, the other represents desire. Their attitude of attentive listening refers to hearing.

The number of this Key, as you have learned, is that of law, of adaptation, of religion, and of man. Psychologically, the Hierophant represents Intuition, which follows reasoning, and adds to it. Intuition is subconscious response to reason, whereby, through laws of association at work below the conscious level, thought-relations which go beyond the results attained by reason are attained. Usually these are perceived by interior hearing. Intuition, it should be noted, means literally "inner tuition."

THE LOVERS

6 | THE LOVERS

X

KEY 6: THE LOVERS (ZAIN)

Zain (Z, value 7) means "sword" or "weapon," suggesting the antithesis of Vav, the nail, because a sword cleaves, cuts, divides, separates. Diversity, contrast, antithesis, distinction, and therefore discrimination, are some of the related ideas. Discrimination implies nice perception, acuteness, sharpness like a sword's edge, sagacity, and so on.

Smelling is the sense attributed to Zain in *The Book of Formation.* The sense of smell has been always associated with keen perception and sagacity. An old Qabalistic maxim says, "Properties are discerned by the nose." Our everyday speech has a number of phrases like "smell out" to suggest approach to truth.

East-Above, the direction assigned to Zain, is the line bounding the eastern side of the top of the Cube of Space, and joining the top face (Above, Mercury) to the eastern face (East, Venus). This line, moreover, joins the top of the vertical line North-East (Emperor) to the top of the vertical line South-East (Hierophant). The combination of East and Above suggests the working together of the subconscious power of creative imagination and the self-conscious power of acute discrimination.

Gemini, the Twins, is the zodiacal sign attributed to Zain. The name of this sign suggests duality, division, and other ideas related to the meaning of the letter. It is difficult to tell twins apart, and to do so requires nice discrimination.

Gemini is ruled by Mercury (Key 1, the Magician), sometimes personified in Egyptian mythology as the jackal-headed Anubis, representing discernment and sagacity because of the jackal's keen sense of smell.

Gemini governs the lungs, collarbones, shoulders, arms and hands (all in pairs). Gemini people are said to be given to inquiry, investigation and experimentation. They often engage in mental pursuits. In our color-scale, Gemini is represented by orange. The corresponding musical tone is D-natural. Gemini is a common sign of the airy triplicity.

Disposing Intelligence is the mode of consciousness assigned to the letter Zain. To dispose is literally "to place apart," to arrange, to distribute, to apportion, to divide. Thus analysis (implied by the meanings of the letter-name, sword), classification, organization, preparation and adjustment are all related to this mode of consciousness. This it is which shows itself in our "disposition," and one's disposition can be modified by right discrimination.

The Lovers is the more usual title. Some pseudo-occultists call this picture "The Two Paths," and say older versions of the symbolism show a man standing between two female figures representing Virtue and Vice. This is wholly erroneous. In old exoteric versions of Tarot there are three figures—a youth and a maiden, facing a crowned woman. These are the Qabalistic Son and Bride combined with the Qabalistic Mother or Queen. The design, aside from its deeper meaning, has obvious reference to marriage. The title intimates the union of opposite but complementary modes of existence. It is also closely related to "Disposing Intelligence." Disposition, affections, temperament, idiosyncrasies, propensities—all these are related to the word "love," as well as to the occult meaning of Key 6.

Our version is essentially the same as Dr. Waite's, and both are based on the unpublished esoteric Tarot. We have been at some pains to clarify certain minor obscurities, but otherwise the symbolism is the same.

The sun overhead has the same general significance as that behind the Fool. It is the great light-source, the dynamo of radiant energy whence all creatures derive their personal forces. Here it is yellow, or golden, instead of white, to show that it is our day-star, the actual physical sun whence we draw not only energy and life, but also, says Ageless Wisdom, potential consciousness. The sun is not merely a center of physical force, a thing in the sky. It is the body of a Being.

The angel is Raphael, angel of air, the element attributed to Gemini, and, in the symbolism of the Roman Church, the particular angel of the planet Mercury. He is also the great archangel of the eastern quarter of the heavens (East-Above). Here he represents superconsciousness, and thus is related also to the Fool. His airy nature is indicated by the color of his skin, the yellow we have associated with air and with Mercury. His violet garment carries out the same idea, because violet is the color-complement of yellow. Another indication of his airy nature is the fact that he is supported by clouds. He is the cosmic Life-Breath, Prana, superconsciousness. His influence descends on both figures below, streaming from his upraised hands.

The mountain in the background combines several meanings. Mountains are symbols of the abode of the gods. Consider Sinai, Olympus, Meru, Fujiyama. Again, they suggest climbing, aspiration, the possibility of attainment. We all have peaks to climb, and the incentive to action, the disposing element in our consciousness which leads to volition, has always in the background this idea of climbing above our present level. Thus the mountain represents what alchemists call the Great Work. Again, a mountain is often a phallic symbol of pregnancy, or gestation, suggesting preparation, organization, and like ideas we have already developed in connection with the letter Zain.

The man at the right of this Key is Adam, namer of things and tiller of the soil. He is also the Magician of Tarot. Behind him is a tree bearing twelve fiery fruits. These are the signs of the zodiac, and each flame is triple, because astrologers subdivide every sign into three parts, or decanates. Thus the tree behind the man is the tree of human life, and its fruits represent the twelve main types, and thirty-six sub-types of personality, or self-conscious life-expression.

The woman at the left is Eve. She is also the High Priestess and the Empress. Behind her is the Tree of Knowledge of Good and Evil. It bears five circular fruits—the five senses. Up the tree climbs the serpent of sensation, because temptation arises from subconscious memory of sensation, or from suggestions based thereon. The serpent is also a symbol of wisdom and of redemption (Moses' serpent in the wilderness), because wisdom and liberation result from the right adaptation of the very forces which, at first, tempt us into mistaken action. Thus Dr. Waite says: "The suggestion in respect of the woman is that she signifies that attraction towards the sensitive life which carries within it the idea of the Fall of Man, but she is rather the working of a Secret Law of Providence than a willing and conscious temptress. It is through her imputed lapse that man shall rise ultimately, and only by her can he complete himself."

In practical psychology the lesson of the picture is plain. The woman looks toward the angel, the man toward the woman. The self-conscious intellectual mind, although it is the determining factor in personal consciousness, does not become directly aware of superconsciousness. Self-consciousness, as the symbolism of Key 1 shows, does receive and transmit the powers of superconsciousness; but conscious awareness of the nature of those powers comes from careful observation of the activities of subconsciousness. Powers are developed within, and the subconscious "within" is the woman. From that within they are educated, or drawn forth, in response to self-conscious impulses, and their manifestation is in the field of self-consciousness (the without). Development comes by response of the inner to the outer. It is the answer of woman to man that peoples the world. It is the response of the interpreting subconsciousness to the observing self-consciousness that peoples the thought-world with ideas. This is a basic law of mental development. Its constructive operation depends on the discriminative exercise of self-conscious powers.

Personal happiness, health and success depend on harmonious co-operation of these two modes of mental activity. To secure this harmony, we must understand that both are expressions of a power superior to either. We must see also that subconsciousness is the mode which, in response to suggestions originated and framed by self-consciousness, brings us into personal relationship with this superior power.

Furthermore, the relationship between self-consciousness and subconsciousness should be one of loving intimacy. Hence the two figures are nude. They veil nothing from each other. This is not the state of affairs with most people. Too often, self-consciousness and subconsciousness are "not on speaking terms." Consciously, we accept this or that idea. Subconsciously, we seek the realization of its opposite. To correct this error, to establish harmony between these two phases of personality, is to have clear, unmixed, unadulterated desires.

Again, since love is the ideal relation between the two modes of consciousness, this picture warns us against any attempt to bully or coerce subconsciousness. Persuade subconsciousness, and it will do anything for you. Endeavor to drive it harshly, and you set into operation the law of reversed effort, so that you get a result just the opposite to that at which you aim.

Discrimination, then, is the key to the establishment of happy co-operation between the two modes of personal consciousness. The burden falls on self-consciousness, because it is the framer of suggestion. If it be careless and lax in observation, or harsh and driving in giving commands to subconsciousness, the results are destructive.

On the other hand, if self-conscious intellect perceives the true relation among the three modes of consciousness, as symbolized in Key 6, it will be able to frame a series of suggestions which will make it the recipient of superconscious guidance, through the agency of subconsciousness.

All that is necessary is to formulate suggestions embodying the idea that subconsciousness can, and does, receive the influence from above, that it can, and does, reflect that influence to self-consciousness. Frame suggestions like these in words of your own. Study the picture, and find words to express its meaning in a formula of auto-suggestion. Your own words are best, and have the most power. You will be amazed and delighted with the result.

THE CHARIOT

7 | THE CHARIOT | ם

XI

KEY 7: THE CHARIOT (CHETH)

Cheth (Ch, and H as in "help," value 8) is pronounced *khayth*. It means a field, and the fence enclosing it. "Fence" suggests enclosure, protection, defense; specific location; an area set apart for cultivation. It also implies shielding, safeguard, refuge, safety. Thus it corresponds to the ideas represented by the words carapace and shell.

The idea of location refers back to "house," or Beth, as does that of shelter. A cultivated field is in contrast to the open country pictured in Key 6. Cultivation, again, is suggested by the gardens of the Magician and the Empress. Again, the enclosure of a particular area by a fence is what happens in the mental world when we define anything, so that Cheth is also related to Heh, considered as the definite article.

Speech is the human function attributed to Cheth by Qabalists. Speech defines. Words are like fences enclosing particular fields of consciousness. The field of speech continually engages the labors of the practical occultist and the applied psychologist. The attribution of speech to Cheth, therefore, indicates that words have preservative and protective power, that right use of language is a means to safety. Extend the meaning of speech from the spoken word to the unspoken words of thought, and you will understand why the wise have always attached so much importance to right speech.

Intelligence of the House of Influence is the Qabalistic name for the mode of consciousness corresponding to Cheth. Literally, it is "consciousness of that which is the abode of inflowing power." It is consciousness of the fact that human personality is like a fenced-in area, wherein universal forces are at work. These forces flow into per-

93

sonality from beyond its boundaries. Taking form in the silent speech of thought, and finding utterance in the spoken word, they flow out through personality into actual expression and manifestation.

East-Below is represented on the Cube of Space by the line or edge connecting the lower ends of the vertical lines North-East and South-East. This edge marks the junction of the eastern and bottom faces of the cube, attributed, respectively, to Daleth and Venus, and to Gimel and the Moon (Keys 3 and 2, The Empress and The High Priestess). Here is an intimation that, though self-conscious elements are involved, the mental activities symbolized by Key 7 are carried on at the subconscious level.

A little self-study will convince you that your thought and speech are largely subconscious in origin. Your vocabulary depends on subconscious associative processes. Your sentences, your style, your figures of speech — all these take shape below the self-conscious level.

Cancer, the Crab, a cardinal, watery sign, is attributed to Cheth. Here we see the connection between the letter-name, "fence," and the crab's hard carapace. Cancer is ruled by the Moon (Key 2, High Priestess), and the planet Jupiter (Key 10, Wheel of Fortune) is exalted therein.

Cancer governs the breast, the chest (a fence of bones) and the stomach. It is a psychic, receptive sign. Its natives are said by astrologers to be endowed with tenacious memory. All this is in accordance with the basic meanings of the letter-name Cheth.

In our color-scale, the tint assigned to Cancer is orange-yellow. The corresponding musical tone is D-sharp or E-flat.

The Chariot is the usual title of Key 7. Sometimes it is *The Charioteer,* which is even better, since the picture, as Dr. Waite says, is really "the King in his triumph, typifying, however, the victory which creates kingship as its natural consequence." Note that the number of the card, 7, is that to which Qabalists assign the idea of Victory.

In the background is a walled city. The wall is a stone fence. The city is a collection of houses, corresponding to the ideas relating to Beth and the Magician. The windows of some of the buildings are clearly shown, indicating that what is represented by Heh and the Emperor is also behind the surface meanings of Key 7. The wall, however, is what most clearly establishes the correspondence of this trump to Cheth, the Fence.

Trees and a river in the middle distance remind us of the symbolism of Key 3, The Empress. This is correct because speech is not only composed of definitions, but also embodies mental imagery (Empress) and gives form to the stream of consciousness. As the river, in Tarot, rises from the watery substance of the robe of the High Priestess, and as trees are associated with the rich fertility of the Empress' garden here, too, is the combination suggested by East-Below (East, Empress, and Below, High Priestess).

The chariot itself is a movable fence, corresponding to the letter Cheth. Its body is a cube, carrying out the symbolism of the cubes whereon the High Priestess and Emperor sit. Moreover, it is of gray stone, so that it combines the notions of wisdom (gray) and of the union of Father and Son suggested by the Qabalistic meaning of ABN, *ehben*, stone.

Surmounting the body of the chariot are four pillars, supporting a starry canopy. The number four is the number of order and measurement. It refers also to the four elements: fire, water, air and earth. Each pillar is divided into two equal parts, reminding us of the Hermetic axiom, "That which is above is as that which is below."

The point of division at the center of each pillar is surrounded by a ring. This is a symbol of Spirit, for the rings are circles, like zero-signs. The idea is that each of the four elements is encircled by the One Spirit.

The starry canopy represents the celestial forces. Their descent into the physical plane through the activity of the four elements is the cause of all external manifestation. Thus the stars in the azure canopy symbolize the correlation of the influences of distant suns and planets, of zodiacal constellations, and of human forces. This canopy therefore represents the forces which surround the earth, and seem to be above us in the sky. It represents also the subtle, metaphysical forces which are above the level of personality. It is therefore a symbol of what Eliphas Levi called "Astral Light."

A shield on the face of the car has the same significance as the letter-name, the wall in the background, and the car itself. The red symbol on the shield is one form of the Hindu lingam-yoni, typifying the union of positive and negative forces in action (red).

In some old Tarot Keys the shield bears the letters .V.T, written with the periods at the left of the letters, to show that they are to be read, like Hebrew, from right to left. So read, they spell the Hebrew word TV, Tav. This is the name of the last letter of the Hebrew alphabet. To an occultist this conveys the same fundamental idea as the lingam-yoni, because the original character for Tav was a cross, combining the vertical masculine line with the feminine horizontal, like the cross on the breast of the High Priestess.

Above the shield is a variation of the Egyptian winged globe. The globe is gold or yellow, suggesting self-consciousness, because, in our color-scale, yellow corresponds to Mercury and the Magician. The wings are blue, like the robe of the High Priestess. They are symbols of aspiration.

The charioteer is crowned, and the crown is surmounted by three golden pentagrams. The pentagram represents mental dominion. Three are shown, because the control we exert over cosmic forces by right use of the power of speech does really extend over three worlds. This detail of symbolism agrees with older forms of Tarot symbolism. In the Rider pack, the diadem is a golden eight-

pointed star, having much the same meaning as the pentagrams, but more particularly emphasizing the idea of the
cosmic order typified in Tarot by the Wheel of Fortune and
its eight spokes. This order is the expression of the super-
vising authority of the One Self, symbolized in Key 17 by a
golden or yellow eight-pointed star.

The charioteer's hair is fair, like that of the Empress and
the Fool. On his shoulders are lunar crescents, indicating
the rulership of the Moon in Cancer. His cuirass is
greenish-yellow, or the color of brass, to show that it symbolizes the protective power of creative imagination,
represented in Tarot by the Empress, inasmuch as brass is a
metal sacred to Venus.

A square on this cuirass represents order and purity by
its shape and color. On it are three black T's, which stand
for the limiting power of Saturn. They also, like the .V.T on
older versions, refer to the letter Tav.

The charioteer's golden belt suggests light, and is ornamented with indistinct signs, among which is one which
is plainly the astrological symbol for Cancer. The position
of this belt suggests the slanting circle of the ecliptic. It
represents Time, and the influences of stellar forces.

The skirt below the cuirass is divided into eight parts,
and is ornamented with geomantic symbols, used in
making magical talismans. They typify dominion over
terrestrial forces.

The charioteer's scepter is surmounted by a figure 8,
combined with a crescent. This is a combination of the
symbol over the Magician's head with the lunar crown of
the High Priestess. Thus the rider's ensign of authority
shows that his dominion is a result of the blending of
the powers of self-consciousness with those of subconsciousness.

Everything about the charioteer suggests that he sums
up all the powers and potencies of the personages who
have preceded him in the series of major trumps. He is
their synthesis. He is the true Self, the Master-power

behind all forms of life-expression. Hence Dr. Waite tells us: "He has led captivity captive; he is conquest on all planes—in the mind, in science, in progress in certain trials of initiation...He is above all things triumph in the mind."

His car symbolizes by its canopy and cubical body the combination of celestial and terrestrial forces. Viewed from the front, it is in the form of an oblong square. Thus it corresponds to the traditional Masonic "form of the lodge." The "lodge" corresponds to the Temple, and we have the highest authority for the doctrine that human personality is the living temple of the Most High. Thus the chariot is truly the "House of Influence," and stands for human personality as the vehicle, or channel of expression, through which the omnipresent SELF manifests its dominion over all things.

The sphinxes which draw the car are an innovation suggested by Eliphas Levi. Older versions of Tarot show horses, which are sometimes joined together, like Siamese twins. The horses are sun-symbols. The sphinxes, combining animal and human attributes, suggest a force common to men and animals. Their contrasting colors are like the contrast between the pillars of the High Priestess. Moreover, the white sphinx wears a beneficient expression, while the features of the black one show a forbidding frown. The white sphinx is a symbol of Mercy, the black one of Severity. Note that their contrasting expressions are similar to those of the human faces in the lunar crescents on the rider's shoulders.

By mythological allusion, the sphinxes represent the senses, which are continually propounding riddles. Here they are shown at rest, thus agreeing with the notion of rest which Hebrew occultism attributes to the number 7.

The yellow wheels of the chariot refer to light-energy, but particularly to specific activities associated in Tarot with the planet Jupiter. This is the planet exalted in the sign Cancer. It is represented in Tarot by the tenth major trump, called "The Wheel of Fortune." Jupiter, astrologers say, rules the circulation of the blood, because it has to do with all forms of rotation, or circular movement.

To this picture we assign the psychological idea, Receptivity-Will. The uninitiated believe their "will" to be something originating in personality. The occultist, without in the least denying the fact that free will is part of our equipment, refuses to believe that "personal" free will exists. For the occultist, all that we mean by "volition" is but a synthesis of innumerable cosmic influences, coming to a focus at a point *within* us.

Hence all the great initiates say, with Jesus, "Of myself I can do nothing." For the same reason Jacob Boehme wrote: "If thou canst, my son, for a while but cease from all thy thinking and willing, then shalt thou hear the unspeakable words of God. . .When thou art quiet and silent, then art thou as God was before nature and creature; thou art that which God then was; thou art that of which he made thy nature and creature: Then thou hearest and seest even with that wherewith God himself saw and heard in thee, before ever thine own willing or thine own seeing began."

The more perfectly we understand that the office of human personality is to serve as a vehicle for cosmic forces, the more freely does the Primal Will behind all manifestation find expression through us. To others we may seem to have very strong personal will. We ourselves will learn from our practice that the strength of our volition is measured by the degree of our willingness to *let* life find unobstructed manifestation through us.

This willingness takes form in thought and word, and the thought itself is unuttered speech. It is a willingness developed through purposeful concentration. Relaxation of body, passivity of mind, one-pointed attention to the real presence in our personal field of the limitless powers of the whole universe, with progressive freedom in the expression of those powers as our dominant purpose — this is the infallible practical formula for triumph in the mind and elsewhere.

Impress subconsciousness again and again with the suggestion that it is the vehicle for Universal Will. Base these suggestions on reason. See that the One Energy enters into all modes of power, celestial and terrestrial. Self-examination will convince you that not the least of your personal actions is anything more or less than a particular manifestation in time and space of some phase of the sum-total of cosmic influences. At our present stage of mental development, perfect conceptions of this truth may be impossible, but reasonable ones we may have at a little expense of observation and reason.

Subconsciousness is the vehicle through which all plans, ideas, designs, inventions and forces enter into the personal field. Thought and speech are potent in moulding subconscious response. Furthermore, because subconsciousness is also the body-building and body-changing power, suggestions of the type here indicated will eventually make profound alterations in physical structure, so that it becomes able to transform into personal activities cosmic forces whose very existence is unsuspected by the greater number of human beings.

Complete receptivity is the secret of the most powerful manifestations of will. Receptivity may be increased by control of language. Herein lies the key to all mighty works of practical occultism, for, as Eliphas Levi says truly, "All magic is in the will."

STRENGTH

8   **STRENGTH**   ל

XII

KEY 8: STRENGTH (TETH)

Teth (Th, as in "the," also T, value 9) means "snake," symbol of what has been known among occultists for ages as the "serpent-power." This was what Moses typified by his brazen image in the wilderness. It is the astral light of Eliphas Levi, the force designated in Theosophy by the term *Fohat*. It is cosmic electricity, the universal life-principle, the conscious energy which takes form as all things, and builds everything from within. The control of this energy in its subhuman forms, by mental means, is the primary secret of practical occultism.

The serpent also symbolizes secrecy, subtlety and wisdom. Thus, in the allegory of Genesis, the tempter is a snake, and the devil is called the "old serpent." This serpent-power is the source of illusion, and thus the "father of lies." Yet, when it is overcome, it becomes the instrumentality of salvation. Again, because the ancients observed that serpents cast their skin, the snake was taken to be a type of reincarnation, regeneration and immortality.

Taste is the sense, and *digestion* the function, assigned to Teth by Qabalists. Literally, digestion is "feeding," and this recalls the familiar serpent biting its own tail, which we have seen in the picture of the Magician. The serpent-power feeds on itself. That is, it is self-sustaining. Scientifically this is correct. The sum-total of the universal conscious energy remains ever the same. It enters into various forms of expression, and these feed on one another. Hence the serpents on the caduceus, or wand of Hermes, represent this law of endless transformation and conversion.

North-Above, the direction assigned to Teth, is represented on the Cube of Space by the upper boundary of the northern face, which is the point of junction between that face and the top of the cube. This line connects the upper points of the line North-East and the line North-West. These are the lines corresponding, respectively, to Key 4, The Emperor, and Key 11, Justice.

The northern face of the cube is represented in Tarot by Key 16, The Tower, symbolizing the planet Mars, and the fiery activity which has for its most obvious manifestation the disintegration of forms. In digestion, the first step is the breaking-up of food by mastication, followed by further disintegration in the chemistry of the stomach and the intestines.

This disintegrating activity, under the conscious self-direction of the mental states typified by Mercury and the Magician (Above), is the basis of practical work in occultism. Until one is wise enough to select and digest the proper sorts of food, he is not ready to experiment with the higher laws of control which enable adepts to perform their mighty works. Corresponding to it, based on the principle expressed in the Hermetic axiom, "As above, so below," is right selection and assimilation of mental food.

Leo, the Lion, a fixed sign of fiery quality, is attributed to the letter Teth. Leo is ruled by The Sun (Key 19). It governs the sides, back, heart and spinal column. It is the sign attributed in Hebrew occultism to the Tribe of Judah. The astrological symbol for Leo resembles a serpent, and the sign, governing the spine, is thus related to the nerve-currents directed upward through the spinal centers in the practice of yoga. In modern astrology Leo is said to be the sign of the exaltation of Neptune (Key 12, The Hanged Man). The color assigned to Leo is yellow. Its musical tone is E-natural.

Intelligence of the Secret of all Spiritual Activities, or *Intelligence of the Secret of Works*, is the mode of consciousness attributed by Qabalists to Teth. Here it should be borne in mind that *all* activities are spiritual, in the literal sense of Spirit, as the cosmic Life-Breath. Part of the secret is the law that all forces and activities whatsoever are transmutations and conversions of the one Conscious Energy. Other phases of this law will be touched upon in our analysis of the symbols of Key 8.

Strength, the title of Key 8, is sometimes given as *Force*, and occasionally, but incorrectly, as *Fortitude*. It is courage only as courage is derived from conscious knowledge of the law typified by the symbolism. The correct titles, Strength or Force, allude to the fiery Life-power which is the source of all human action.

The yellow background of the picture agrees with the color attributed to Leo in our scale. In the distance is a mountain-peak, like the one shown in Key 6, and having the same meanings. In contrast to the urban aspect of Key 7, the scene here is an uninhabited plain. It is a plain in a valley, suggesting the level of actual existence, but the absence of houses indicates that the conditions here are those of nature, apart from human artifice.

The woman's yellow hair identifies her with the Empress, so that we may understand her to represent creative imagination and the subconscious generation of mental imagery. Instead of a wreath, she wears a crown of flowers, indicating that, at the point of development shown by Key 8, the forces of organic life are nearer to fruition.

Over her head is the same horizontal 8 that hovers over the head of the Magician. It has the same meanings. It further intimates that something of the Magician's quality has been transferred to the woman. It indicates the fact that subconsciousness receives the impress of self-conscious mental states, and is modified by self-conscious selectivity and initiative. Even as the outcome of the digestive processes, themselves governed by subconsciousness, depends on our conscious selection of food, and our conscious attention to the preliminary work of mastication, so does the outcome of subconscious operations in general depend for good or ill on the selection and direction which are the particular business of the self-conscious plane of mind. Note, in this connection, that on the Cube of Space the line North-Above is at the top of the cube, or at the level of the upper surface, which is assigned to Key 1, The Magician.

The unornamented white robe of the woman signifies purity, in the strictest sense of that word, which means "freedom from mixture." Because white is the color assigned to Kether, the Crown, which is the uppermost circle on the Qabalistic diagram of the Tree of Life, this color, wherever it appears in Tarot symbolism, relates to the pure spiritual influence of the Primal Will.

Around her waist is a chain of roses, twisted (though this detail is not very clear in the picture) so as to form another figure 8, and Dr. Waite says the woman leads the lion by this chain of flowers. It signifies artistic adaptation (chain) of desire (roses). When we learn how to weave our desires together into a chain, rejecting all desires which are incompatible with our main purpose, and co-ordinating those we do decide upon as fitting to our purpose, we shall be able to make wonderful applications of creative imagination to the control and direction of the serpent-power.

The lion, as king of beasts, represents all subhuman forces, all subhuman expressions of the cosmic vital electricity. The king stands for all his subjects. His color refers to the alchemical Red Lion, symbol of Sulphur, purified and sublimated by its amalgamation with Mercury. This is exactly the idea hinted at by the attribution of North-Above to this Key, inasmuch as the alchemical "sulphur" has to do with a fiery, electro-magnetic potency common to the Sun, ruler of Leo, and to Mars (North), and this potency is directed by self-consciousness (Mercury, Above). The lion also confirms the attribution of Key 8 to Leo. You will remember that some mention of this was made in Chapter 3.

The woman tames the lion. In Dr. Waite's version, she shuts his mouth. In the B.O.T.A. version reproduced herewith, as in all the older versions, she opens it. This is preferable, since "to open the mouth" is to make articulate, to give speech to, and whatever has the power of speech is assimilated with humanity and impressed by human thought. When we assimilate the hostile, destructive, dangerous, wild forces in nature to the uses of mankind, we add to those forces the quality of human consciousness. Thus electricity, the flaming thunder-bolt, tamed and modified by man is now, as Eliphas Levi predicted, what gives to human speech "a universal reverberation and success."

The meaning of the picture should now be plain. The Great Secret is the law that subconsciousness is at all times in control of every subhuman manifestation of cosmic energy. The extent of this control is far greater than is usually supposed. Every force in nature, down to those of the inorganic mineral kingdom, is within range of this subconscious direction. Actually, it is because of this that man is able to extend his dominion over the forces of his environment, even to the point where he may bring into actual manifestation chemical elements which, so far as we are able to determine from spectroscopic analysis of the stars, exist nowhere but on this planet. Neptunium and plutonium, the elements brought into active manifestation by atomic fission, are truly thought-born. Their genesis began with self-conscious mathematical analysis of the properties of matter. This analysis was then made the basis of imagination and invention. The new elements began their existence in man's mind, and became actual things in the external world as the result of mind-directed and mind-conceived works of man. Even greater things than these are possible for the adept who has mastered his own emotions and desires.

Subconsciousness always directs the activities of the subhuman forces of nature. This is true whether the action of those forces be hostile or friendly to man. Subconsciousness, in turn, is always amenable to impressions originating at the self-conscious level of mentation.

What matters, therefore, is the kind of patterns we set. Our mental patterns are determined by self-conscious interpretation of experience. Let observation and attention (the Magician) be faulty, superficial, negative or fearful and the resulting sequence of subconscious reactions is bound to be destructive. Then the spoken word and unuttered speech of thought (the Chariot) will be vehicles for a destructive pattern, and we shall set wild beasts at our own vitals.

Change the pattern, and you change the result. Make it accurate, profound, courageous, positive. Then you tame the lion, and he becomes your servant. This, indeed, is the secret of all spiritual activities, the secret of strength, the secret of ultimate mastery. Your personal application of this secret to your own life will change everything for the better. Carry it further, into all your social relations, and you will become one of that increasing number of builders of a new, free world that shall realize the glory of the Eternal Splendor of the Limitless Light.

THE HERMIT

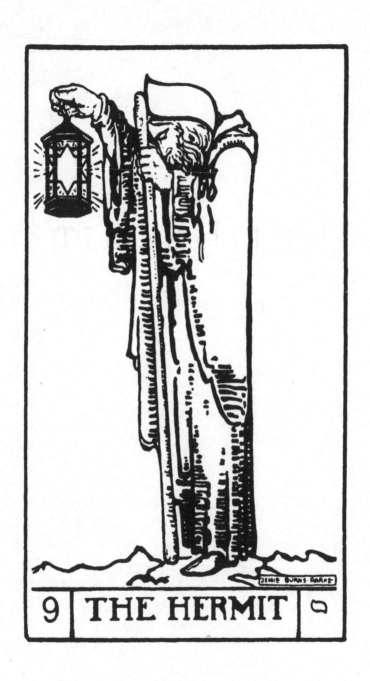

9 | THE HERMIT

XIII

KEY 9: THE HERMIT (YOD)

Yod (I, J, Y, value 10) means the hand of man. It is the open hand, in contradistinction to Kaph, the closed one, which follows it in the alphabet. Yod indicates power, means, direction; skill, dexterity; but it is the sign rather of tendency, aptitude, inclination, predisposition or potency than of actual activity. In the religious symbolism of the world the open hand is everywhere and at all times a type of beneficence, and of the freedom of the Supreme Spirit.

In the Qabalah, this letter has special importance because it is the initial letter of the Tetragrammaton, IHVH, and the initial letter also of the word IChIDH, Yekhidah, the term used in the Wisdom of Israel to designate the INDIVISIBLE ONE, the Supreme SELF, having its abode or seat in Kether, the Crown, at the top of the Tree of Life. Qabalists, moreover, say that the upper point of the letter refers to Kether, the Primal Will, while the body of the letter represents the second Sephirah, Chokmah or Wisdom.

The sense of *Touch* is that which is attributed to Yod, and the same letter, in Qabalah, corresponds to the function of *Coition*, in which the sense of touch is particularly active. Esoterically, the letter Yod corresponds to the experience of union with the Supreme SELF, the true I AM of the cosmos. This experience, intensely blissful, is often compared by occult writers, both ancient and modern, to the intense physical ecstasy of the sex embrace. Prudes may quarrel with this comparison. Let them read the Song of Solomon, the mystical poetry of Persian Sufis, or some of the narratives of Christian mystical experience, and they will learn that some of the best minds the human race has ever produced have not scrupled to employ intensely erotic imagery in their endeavors to describe the bliss of union with the ONE.

North-Below is the direction attributed by Qabalists to Yod. On the Cube of Space it is the lower boundary of the northern face, and the northern boundary of the lower face. It joins the lower ends of the vertical lines North-East (the Emperor) and North-West (Justice). One reason for this attribution is that the destruction of error symbolized by Key 16 (North) is one of the elements of mystic experience. Furthermore, that experience depends on certain transformations of the Mars-force in the physical body, and these transformations are effected by subconsciousness (Below). Again, mystic experience is the supreme expression of subconscious processes of memory and association (High Priestess, Below). When we most perfectly remember ourselves we experience this blissful merging of personal consciousness with the universal. The color assigned to Virgo is yellow-green. Its musical tone is F-natural.

Virgo, the Virgin, a mutable or common earthy sign, is attributed to the letter Yod. It is ruled by Mercury (Key 1, the Magician), and is also the sign in which Mercury is exalted. Virgo is dominated, therefore, by self-conscious initiative, and represents the state in which the highest manifestation of self-consciousness is experienced.

This state is what the Bible calls "heaven." Therefore Jesus said that in heaven there is neither marriage, nor giving in marriage, because in the blissful state of union there is no sense of "otherness," or separation. This corresponds to the idea of virginity connected with the sign. In the state of consciousness we are now considering, all distinctions of separate personality, and, consequently, all distinctions of sex, are completely obliterated.

Astrologers say Virgo rules the intestines, where digestion is completed, and where the final selection is made between assimilable material and what is rejected as waste. In certain forms of occult practice, concealed under the veils of alchemy, the assimilation of solar energy from food by the lacteals in the small intestine is tremendously increased. To this practice we may refer alchemical references to the First Matter as "virgin's milk," prepared under the regimen of Mercury; to the process of putrefaction symbolized by a black dragon (the convolutions of the intestines in the darkness of the abdominal cavity); and to the fact that, in its visible aspect, the First Matter is a thing accounted by all men to be the vilest thing on earth.

Intelligence of Will is the mode of consciousness attributed to the letter Yod. Say the Qabalists: "It prepares all created beings, each individually, for the demonstration of the existence of the primordial glory." This demonstration is the experience hitherto described. The primordial glory is that of the Supreme SELF.

The word translated above as "Will" means primarily "delight," and has, for supplementary meanings, "pleasure, intent, purpose, determination." Thus we find that all descriptions of mystic experience agree that it is first-hand knowledge of an ineffable glory, of an unspeakable bliss, and of an intensely certain and definite, though incommunicable, knowledge of the meaning and tendency of the cosmic life-process. In this experience the question, "What is this all about?" is settled, once and for all. In it, too, the knowledge that there can be but one Free Will in the universe, of which Free Will all things and creatures are personal expressions, is a knowledge established forever.

The Hermit is a title referring to a passage in the Qabalah which says: "Yod is above all (symbolizing the Father), and with Him is none other associated." A hermit lives alone, isolated. The picture shows him alone, standing on a snowy mountain-peak, far above the climbing travelers for whom he holds aloft his lantern as a beacon.

His white beard shows that he is the "Most Holy Ancient One," identified with the Primal Will. His gray, cowled robe suggests another Qabalistic title for the

The Tarot

ONE—"Concealed with all Concealment." He is the Source of all, yet is he also the goal of all endeavor. Every practice in occult training aims at the union of personal consciousness with the Cosmic Will which is the Causeless Cause of all particular manifestations.

At first it may puzzle you to account for the fact that a letter assigned to the direction North-Below should be symbolized by a man standing on a height. Remember the axiom, "That which is above is as that which is below." Remember also that such words as cause, source, origin, etc., are related to that which is basic, fundamental, and therefore *at the bottom* of things.

Again, 9, the number of this Key, is a number of completion, as you learned in Chapter 2; but in the same chapter you were told that this completion is inseparable from, and really identical with, the primary Idea which begins the process of manifestation. The meaning should be even clearer after you have considered the analogies between 9, the number of the Hermit, and 0, the number of the Fool.

The sign which precedes all manifestation is 0, and 9, final figure of the digital series, denotes completion, perfection, realization. The only perfect Being must be the Absolute, and the Absolute is not only No-Thing (the Fool) but is also That which is completely alone (Hermit). Perfection is prior to, and behind, all manifestation, yet it is also beyond and above all things.

9 therefore represents the Absolute as the Goal of existence, while 0 typifies the same Absolute as the Source of all. Consequently, in Tarot 0 is a youth, looking upward, in the morning light; but 9 is a bearded ancient, looking down, at night. The Hermit and the Fool are two aspects of that which is the Foundation (9) of all manifestation. The Hermit is the Ancient One, above all things, yet supporting all. He precedes everything, and, when considered in that aspect, is forever young (the Fool); yet He will continue when all else has passed away, and He is the term of all our hopes.

114

He stands in darkness, because what is behind our personifications of the Supreme Reality is darkly incomprehensible to our intellects. The darkness represents also the hidden, interior, subconscious field of the Divine Operation. The peak whereon he stands is snow-capped because to us this Ancient One is an abstraction, cold, and far removed from the warmth of everyday life. Yet he himself carries his own light, and holds it aloft for the benefit of those who toil upward toward him. It is the light of a golden, six-rayed star, and its interlaced triangles are symbols of union. The six points of the star hint also at Virgo, sixth sign in the zodiacal series.

Although the Hermit seems to be alone, he is really the Way-shower, lighting the path for climbing multitudes below. He has no need to climb, hence his staff is held in his left hand. The staff is one of the implements of the Magician, and corresponds to the archetypal world.

When we reason about it, the Causeless Cause seems afar off — a cold, isolated abstraction. In truth it is intimately related to every circumstance in our daily personal experience. It is the substance, the power, the consciousness expressed in the least of our experiences. It is the source of all our personal light and wisdom. It is the objective of all our aspirations.

The Hermit is the Supreme Will, the cosmic, eternal urge to freedom. Union with that will is the highest result of the operation of the law that subconsciousness responds to the initiative and to the suggestions of self-consciousness. Only through the working of the subconscious body-transforming powers may our bodies undergo the subtle changes which make them fit vehicles for union with the Supreme Spirit.

This is why Mercury, ruler of Virgo, is also exalted or sublimated in that sign. Mercury is the Magician, and self-training in right interpretation of experience, in concentration, in the manipulation of subconsciousness, is what bears fruit finally in union with what is pictured here as the Hermit. In this union the sense of personal "self" is lost, and one knows nothing but the I AM. Hence occult teachings frequently call this experience "Isolation," exactly what the title of Key 9 implies.

Psychologically, this is the state of being conscious that all volition is universal, rather than personal. It includes first-hand knowledge of the law of the eternal freedom of the true SELF. This carries with it the perception that the idea of "personal" will, that is, of will originating in, or inhering in, personality, must be an illusion.

This consciousness, "the demonstration of the existence of the primordial glory," is the basis of the mighty works of adepts, the foundation for the miracles which are the evidences of genuine sainthood. Thus, and also because it is consciousness of the true basis of all manifestation, the Hermit bears the number which Hebrew occultism associates with "Basis" or "Foundation."

This number 9, it should be remarked, is also the number which Qabalists ascribe to the reproductive organs of Adam Qadmon, the Archetypal Man. For all sages are agreed that though Intelligence of Will seems to be the outcome of personal effort and aspiration, it is really the final stage of a work initiated and carried on by the Life-power itself. That work, they say, is one in which the Heavenly Man reproduces himself in the image of the earthly. Herein some of our readers may find a clue to the inner meaning of the doctrine that the Christos is "begotten, not made."

THE WHEEL
OF FORTUNE

10 VHEEL OF FORTUNE

XIV

KEY 10: THE WHEEL OF FORTUNE (KAPH)

Kaph (C, as in "core," or K, value 20; as a final letter, 500) means primarily "a curve," which should be remembered in connection with the fact that in Tarot a wheel is attributed to this letter. Kaph is the hand of the man in the act of grasping. To grasp is to hold, to comprehend, to master. What can be grasped mentally is intelligible, clear, explicit, positive, definite, precise. These ideas, it will be seen, are in sharp contrast to the ineffability and abstractness of those which are related to Yod and the Hermit.

Wealth and Poverty are the pair of opposites attributed to the double letter Kaph. These are the extremes of property, the external signs of one's grasp of circumstances.

West, the direction attributed to Kaph, is represented on the diagram of the Cube of Space by the face nearest the observer. At the place of sunset, West symbolizes the completion of a day, or of a cycle of manifestation — the closing of a circle or round of expression. This is in agreement with the symbol of the closed hand. The close of the day's work, with the setting sun, is related to such ideas as completion, accomplishment, mastery, success, and the like. Free Masons will remember that the officer who sits in the West is charged with paying the wages of the workmen.

Again, it is written, "Westward the course of empire takes its way," for the facts of human history exemplify the principles of cosmic law. Thus, too, the Occidental world is the world in which practical grasp of material powers is the characteristic mark of success, in contrast to the Orient, where a man's wealth is more likely to be reckoned in terms of his understanding of those laws of mental germination typified in Tarot by Key 3, The Empress, to which the direction East is attributed.

Jupiter, the planet attributed to Kaph, rules the zodiacal signs Sagittarius (Key 14, Temperance) and Pisces (Key 18, The Moon). Jupiter is also exalted in Cancer (Key 7, The Chariot, wherein this planet's influence is symbolized by the wheels). Jupiter is called the "Lord of Fortune," or the "Greater Fortune," in contrast to Venus (The Empress), whom astrologers denominate the "Lesser Fortune." In astrology Jupiter signifies bankers, judges and theologians or religious dignitaries—that is, men who have a firm grasp on the comprehensive, lucid statement of ideas, and knowledge of the application of ideas in the administration of practical affairs. Jupiter is said to govern the circulation of the blood, and circular motion generally. The color assigned to this planet in our scale is violet. The musical tone corresponding is B-flat or A-sharp.

Intelligence of Conciliation, or *Rewarding Intelligence of Those Who Seek*, is the Qabalistic name for the mode of consciousness attributed to the letter Kaph. Conciliation is the adjustment of differences, the establishment of harmony and order, and thus is distinctly Jupiterian. This mode of consciousness is what brings perception of the law which fulfils the promise, "Seek, and ye shall find." Conciliation implies concord, agreement, sympathy, peace, amity, tranquility. The law here shown is that which reconciles apparent differences, that which enables us to harmonize the elements of existence, that which leads to the winning over of seemingly antagonistic forces, that which conduces to peace and prosperity.

The title of Key 10, *The Wheel of Fortune*, combines the ideas of rotation, cyclicity, sequence, whirling motion, simultaneous ascent and descent (evolution and involution), and so on, with the ideas of fortune, destiny, chance, fate, necessity, probability, and the like. Occult teaching emphatically asserts that what seems to be chance—whether absence of purpose or absence of design—is really the working of unalterable law. The rotation of circumstance appears to be accidental, but is not really so.

Every effect is the consequence of preceding causes, and the better we grasp this law of sequence and cyclicity, the greater our command over subsequent events. There is periodicity in everything.

The affairs of men, and those of nations, have a rhythm, a regularity, a steadiness of beat which enables the wise to read the meaning of the present in the history of the past, and makes it possible to forecast the events of the future from close examination of present tendencies. The wheel, moreover, is a symbol of progress, advancement, improvement, and so represents the march of culture, civilization, and amelioration which, in occultism, is called the Great Work.

The design of the tenth major trump, in this version of Tarot and in the Rider pack, is adapted from Eliphas Levi's diagram of the Wheel of Ezekiel, in his *Ritual of the Sanctum Regnum*. At the corners of the card, seated on clouds, are the mystical animals mentioned in Ezekiel 1:10 and in Revelation 4:7. They correspond to the fixed signs of the zodiac: the bull to Taurus; the lion to Leo; the eagle to Scorpio; the man to Aquarius. The numbers of these signs in the zodiacal series are 2, 5, 8 and 11, adding to 26, the number of IHVH. In this name, I is represented by the lion, the first H by the eagle, the V by the man, and the final H by the bull. Thus the "living creatures" typify the fixed, eternal modes of the One Reality, which, so to say, remain permanent in contrast to the flux and reflux symbolized by the turning wheel. That which was, is, and shall be remains ever the same in itself, and the whole sequence and rotation of events goes on *within* it.

The wheel is the symbol of the whole cycle of cosmic expression, and is also an emblem of any particular series of events. Its center, or pivot, is the archetypal world; the inner circle is the creative world, the middle circle the formative world, and the outer circle the material world. The eight spokes are like the eight-pointed star, in Key 17, and represent the universal radiant energy. This central circle is the same as the symbol of the Life-Breath, ten times repeated on the dress of the Fool.

On the spokes of the wheel in the circle representing the formative world are the alchemical symbols of mercury (above), sulphur (to the right), and salt (to the left). These correspond to the three *gunas* of yoga philosophy: sattva (mercury), rajas (sulphur) and tamas (salt). At the bottom of the same circle is one of the alchemical symbols for dissolution, identical with the astrological symbol for Aquarius. Mercury is consciousness, sulphur is passion and activity, salt is ignorance and inertia. Dissolution is said to be the fundamental process of the Great Work.

A yellow serpent, its wavy movement suggesting vibration, and its color that which is assigned to light, to the planet Mercury (Key 1, The Magician) and to the sign Leo (Key 8, Strength) in one of the ancient occult color-scales, descends on the left side of the wheel. Its descent represents the involution of the cosmic radiant energy into the conditions of name and form. It is the serpent-power represented by the letter Teth, and so connected with the sign Leo and Key 8. It is also the force which descends through the Magician to his garden, and this force bears the message or impulse of the cosmic will.

Hermanubis (Hermes-Anubis), jackal-headed Egyptian god, rises on the right side of the wheel, to represent the evolution of consciousness from lower to higher forms. His jackal's head represents intellectuality. His red color typifies desire and activity. He symbolizes the average level of our present human development of consciousness. Beyond and above him is a segment of the wheel which only a few humans being have, as yet, traversed.

The sphinx typifies the real Self of man, behind the veil of personality. It is known by the unfoldment of inner senses corresponding to the outer ones. When this unfoldment comes, we become aware of the One Thing which transcends personality. This One Thing is the propounder of the riddles of existence. It remains motionless while the wheel turns. Its blue color relates it to memory, the basic function of subconsciousness, as if to emphasize the idea that the highest self-knowledge is really self-recollection.

On the wheel, in the circle representing the material world, are the letters TARO counterchanged with the Hebrew letters spelling IHVH. In Hebrew values, the letters of TARO make the number 671, important in Qabalah as the number of certain titles of Malkuth, the Kingdom. As the value of IHVH is 26, the total numeration of the eight letters on the wheel is 697, and the digits of 697 add to 22, a number associated with the circle or wheel from time immemorial, and the numbers of letters in the Hebrew alphabet, symbolized by the major trumps of Tarot.

By transposition, the letters of TARO may be arranged to make the following five words: ROTA TARO ORAT TORA ATOR. "Ator" is an old Latin form of the name of the Egyptian goddess Hathor. Thus this rather barbarous Latin sentence may be translated, "The Wheel of Tarot speaks the Law of Hathor (the Law of Nature)."

Psychologically, this Tarot Key refers to the law of periodicity in mental activity, whereby mental states have a tendency to recur in definite rhythms. It is the law, also, of the involution of undifferentiated conscious energy, and its evolution through a series of personalized forms of itself. Finally, the Wheel of Fortune is the Tarot symbol of the law of cause and consequence which enables us to be certain of reaping what we have sown.

JUSTICE

11   **JUSTICE**   ל

XV

KEY 11: JUSTICE (LAMED)

Lamed (L, value 30) means, as a verb, "to teach, to instruct." As a noun, identical with the Hebrew letter-name, Lamed signifies "an ox-goad." Since the ox, in this alphabet, is Aleph, Lamed stands for that which urges and guides the manifestation of the cosmic power represented in Tarot by the Fool.

Now, this cosmic power is all-pervading and all-embracing. Consequently, there can be no other power, outside it, to set it in motion and direct its course. We must understand, then, that the letter Lamed stands for something *within* the Life-power. It represents an inward urge or drive, and an inward capacity for self-direction.

In *The Book of Formation* the special function assigned to Lamed is *Work* or *Action*. This is also the basic meaning of the Sanskrit term *Karma*.

North-West is the direction properly belonging to Lamed. In the first edition of this book, it was incorrectly given as South-West, as in some versions of *The Book of Formation*, but subsequent research and comparison of ancient texts has shown the inaccuracy of this attribution. The line North-West on the Cube of Space is the vertical line at the junction of the north and west sides of the cube. The upper point of this line is the corner at which the lines North-Above and West-Above are joined. The lower point of this line is the corner at which the lines North-Below and West-Below are joined. The fiery, exciting nature of the planet Mars, connected with the north side of the Cube of Space, is thus combined in this attribution with the expansive and rotary quality associated with Jupiter. See Keys 16 and 10 for the Tarot symbolism.

Libra, the Scales, is a cardinal, airy sign. It is ruled by

The Tarot

Venus (Key 3, The Empress), and is the sign in which Saturn (Key 21, The World) is exalted. Our subconscious deductions from experience are the seeds of Karma, and are actually the basis of all our activities. From them we gain instruction and knowledge. Furthermore, the highest manifestation of the restrictive, concrete, definitive power of Saturn is brought about through the operation of the law symbolized by Key 11.

Libra governs the kidneys, loins and lumbar region of the spine. Astrologers say that Librans love justice, order and harmony. Their Venusian quality is shown by their love of beauty and culture. They are said to have keen sense of comparison, foresight, and acute perceptions. The Libran color is green. The corresponding musical tone is F-sharp or G-flat.

Faithful Intelligence is the special mode of consciousness attributed by Qabalists to the letter Lamed. The Hebrew for "faithful" is AMN, Amen, which we say as a confirmatory expression at the end of prayers. This word is closely related to the Sanskrit AUM, or Om, and to the name of the Egyptian god Amun, often written Amen. In the Qabalah we are told that "spiritual virtues are deposited in the Faithful Intelligence, and augment therein." Here is the very idea of the ripening of perception and interpretation into motives for action, so familiar to occultists as a fundamental meaning of Karma.

Justice, the title of Key 11, signifies the active administration of law. It also makes us think of balance, poise, exactitude, accuracy, impartiality, equity, and the like.

The central figure of the design is a conventional personification of Justice, but she wears no blindfold. Her yellow hair, like that of the Empress, identifies her as Venus. So does her green cape, because in our color-scale, green is attributed to Venus. We may identify her also with the woman who tames the red lion in Key 8, and it should be remembered that, in the exoteric Tarot, Key 8 is Justice and Key 11 is Strength. This blind does not mislead those

128

who know the attributions of the signs of the zodiac to the letters of the alphabet. Just why it was employed at all may be difficult to understand now. Yet it does serve to emphasize the fact that Keys 8 and 11 represent two aspects of the operation of a single power, which power is the creative imagination symbolized by the Empress.

In the B.O.T.A. version, the woman's dress has an ornamental collar, displaying a blue-violet T-cross. This, by shape and color, refers to the exaltation of Saturn in Libra. So does the T-cross which is the hilt of the uplifted sword.

The red robe is the color of Mars, complement of the green of Venus. The Greek myth concerning the clandestine love-affair of Mars and Venus intimates that action (Mars) and imagination (Venus) are always related. Mars rules the tonicity of the muscles. Consequently all work or action, the function attributed in Qabalah to Libra, depends on this Mars force in the muscles.

Underneath the red robe, showing at the sleeves, is a blue undergarment. This is the color of the High Priestess, and her number, 2, results from adding the digits of 11, the number of Justice. For all imagination is based on memory.

In the Rider pack, Justice wears a crown, showing three turrets, and ornamented with a square jewel. The three turrets and the four sides of the square give the number 7, the Qabalistic number of the Sphere of Venus on the Tree of Life. In the B.O.T.A. version the square is white, and contains a red circle. Since 22 is the conventional arithmetical symbol for any circle, and a square stands for 4, the two together, like the Masonic square and compass, represent the number 26, which is the value of the divine name IHVH (Jehovah).

The golden scales in the woman's left hand are a subtle hint that solar energy, or light, for which the ancient symbol is gold, may be used as an instrument whereby to weigh and measure action. This fact was well known to occultists in the day Tarot was invented, and modern science confirms this by making the speed of light, and also its mass, the basis for calculations which demonstrate the electrical nature of all so-called "matter." These same calculations have led to the discovery of atomic fission, which will undoubtedly bring about the revolution of chemical and physical science predicted in 1859 by Eliphas Levi. This discovery will also give the whole human race new standards of action, and will make possible in the affairs of men a closer approximation to ideal justice.

The yellow background refers to the element of air, since Libra is an airy sign. Violet, the color of the curtains, is referred to Jupiter and the Wheel of Fortune, to suggest that the veils of mechanism (Key 10) conceal from the uninitiated that the whole universe is permeated by the Life-Breath of Spirit, symbolized by yellow.

The throne of the woman has also, stretched between its two pillars, a violet veil. Pillars and veil are reflections of the ideas suggested by similar symbols in the picture of the High Priestess.

The sword is of steel, a metal attributed to Mars. It is an indication that all action destroys as well as builds. We may take it, likewise, to represent the elimination of all waste and hesitancy from wisely directed action, and to be a reference to the idea of discrimination represented by Zain, the sword, in the Hebrew alphabet and by Key 6 of Tarot.

The general meaning of Key 11 is that education (ox-goad) has equilibration for its aim. It requires, therefore, the elimination of useless, outworn forms (sword, and attribution of Libra to the kidneys). Education is completed by action and work. Merely hearing the word, or reading it, is not true education. Action is required, and action is motivated by subconscious response to self-conscious observation and concentration.

Psychologically, this picture illustrates the law of poise and self-direction. A balanced personality is faithful, constant and confident, because right use of reason has established enduring certainty as to the just outcome of all activities. For a practical occultist this card signifies: (1) You really know only when you have acted; (2) Equilibration, mental and physical, demands the elimination of waste, the getting rid of "excess baggage."

The Hanged Man

| 12 | **HANGED MAN** | ל |

XVI

KEY 12: THE HANGED MAN (MEM)

Mem (M, value 40. Value as final letter in a word, 600). This is the second of the three mother letters of the Hebrew alphabet. Its name means literally "seas," but, like many plurals in Hebrew, it designates a general idea, in this instance, "water." In this connection, we may note that alchemists call water "the mother, seed, and root of all minerals."

In ancient books neither direction nor planet is assigned to this letter. In the Cube of Space, however, it corresponds to the inner axis of the cube connecting the center of the eastern face with the center of the western face. Moreover, the final form of the letter Mem shares with the letter Tav the attribution to the innermost center of the Cube of Space, and to this attribution part of the symbolism of Key 12 refers. In modern astrology, however, Neptune corresponds to Mem. The color assigned to this planet is pale-blue, and the corresponding musical tone is G-sharp or A-flat.

Water, the element represented by Mem, is the first mirror. Water reflects images upside-down, and this idea is carried out by the symbolism and title of Key 12, which is a symbol of reflected life, of life in image, of life in the forms taken by the occult "water," or cosmic substance.

Hanged Man, the title, means occultly, "suspended mind," because "man" and "mind" are from the same Sanskrit root, and this fact was known to the occultists who invented Tarot. The title refers also to the utter dependence of human personality upon the cosmic life.

In the Rider pack the youth hangs from a T-cross, but it is a cross of living wood, to symbolize the cosmic life. It also represents the letter Tav, and in the B.O.T.A. Tarot the gallows from which the Hanged Man is suspended is shaped like a Hebrew Tav, as it is in all versions of this Key except the Rider pack.

In 1918 I received from an occult correspondent the following explanation of the Hanged Man:

"The correct geometrical figure concealed by the Hanged Man is a cross, surmounting a water triangle. It signifies the multiplication of the tetrad by the triad. This is the number 12. The door, Daleth, is the vehicle of the tetrad, for it is the Great Womb also; and the head of the Hanged Man reflected therein is the LVX, in manifestation as the Logos. He is Osiris, Sacrifice, and Yod-Heh-Shin-Vav-Heh, Yeheshua."

This is explanation enough for an advanced occultist, but requires some elaboration for the purposes of this book. It is evident that the legs of the Hanged Man form a cross, and that lines drawn from his elbows to the point formed by his hair will form the sides of a reversed triangle having his arms for its base.

The cross is the number 4, and the triangle is the number 3. The multiplication of these two numbers results in 12, which, because it is the number of signs in the zodiac, represents a complete cycle of manifestation.

The inverted triangle is one of the ancient ways of writing the letter Daleth, which corresponds to the Empress, numbered 3 in Tarot. She is what Hindus call Prakriti, the Great Womb of cosmic substance, the generatrix of all forms.

By a similar numerical correspondence, the crossed legs of the Hanged Man may be taken to represent the Emperor, since they indicate the number 4. Thus they are red, the color of action, and also the color of fire, the particular quality of the sign Aries, typified by the Emperor.

The upper garment of the Hanged Man is blue, color of water, and of the robe of the High Priestess, symbol of the universal mind-stuff. It has two pockets shaped like crescents, and colored silver. Ten silver buttons refer to the ten Sephiroth by their number, and by their material suggest that manifested life is a reflection of the One Life.

The belt and the braid down the front of the Hanged Man's jacket form a cross, and the edging of his collar is so drawn that if we could see it all it would form a circle. Thus this part of the Hanged Man's dress forms an inverted Venus symbol.

"The head of the Hanged Man . . . is LVX, in manifestation as the Logos," means that his head, by its white hair, suggests identity with the Emperor and the Hermit. He is the Ancient of Days, reflected into the incarnate life of personality. One of the old occult names for the One Life is LVX, which is Latin for "Light," and this word is also an occult reference to the Hebrew name "Adonai," or "Lord." For the numeral values of the letters L, V and X in Roman numerals are, respectively, 50, 5 and 10. Their sum is 65, the numeration of the Hebrew name ADNI, Adonai, Lord. The One Light is the Word which is made flesh, and is then represented by the esoteric Hebrew spelling of the name Jesus, i.e.: IHShVH, Yod-Heh-Shin-Vav-Heh, Yeheshua, because Jesus was named after the Hebrew hero, Joshua.

These, however, are meanings of the picture which will not be likely to seem as important as they really are until the student has made considerable advance along the occult path. Fortunately, there are other meanings, less withdrawn from ordinary ways of thinking, but by no means less important. To these we shall devote the rest of this chapter.

Here is a man turned upside down, inverted, in a position contrary to that in which we find most people. Tradition says, by the way, that St. Peter was crucified in this position, and the tradition may have more than a hint for us, when combined with the idea that Peter is the "rock of foundation." For the basis of the occult approach to life, the foundation of the everyday practice of a person who lives the life of obedience to esoteric law, is the reversal of the more usual ways of thinking, speaking and doing. Hence Jacob Boehme said, you may remember, that the great secret is "to walk in all things contrary to the world."

The same idea is represented by the garments of the Hanged Man. His legs are red, color of fire, and his jacket is blue, color of water. These elements are as opposite as light and darkness, as contrary as black and white. Thus opposition is plainly symbolized by the clothes, as well as by the position of the figure.

This does not mean outspoken antagonism to others. On the contrary, such a spirit is precisely the way of the world which occultists endeavor to avoid. Hence this picture is associated with the letter Mem, of which Qabalists say, "Mem is mute, like water." Silent, unostentatious reversal of one's own way of life, combined with perfect tolerance of the ways of other people, is the method of the practical occultist.

In what, then, does the reversal consist? Primarily, in a reversal of thought, in a point-of-view which is just the opposite to that accepted by most persons. At first there may seem to be no practical advantage in this, but just consider. One need only look about him to see that most people are sick, that most people are in trouble, that most people cannot get along with themselves or the world. Does it not become evident, then, that most people are in trouble because they have somehow put the cart before the horse in their practice of life?

In this scientific age we know that everything is an expression of the working of the law of cause and effect. Is it not plain, therefore, that the miseries afflicting most people are the result of their negative use of the law? For every moment of a human life is some special application of the law, and the outcome depends wholly on whether the application be positive or negative.

Practical psychology shows us the potency of ideas. It demonstrates conclusively the truth that thoughts are the seeds of speech and action, that interpretations are the patterns for experience, that what happens to us is what we have selected, whether the selection be conscious and intentional, or unconscious and unpremeditated. Thus, in practical psychology, the emphasis is upon the importance of a changed view-point, and this change is no less than a total reversal.

Every idea we considered in our study of Key 11 points to the central theme of the Hanged Man. This is that every human personality is completely dependent upon the All, here symbolized by the tree. As soon as this truth is realized, the only logical and sensible course of conduct is a complete self-surrender. This surrender begins in the mind. It is the submission of the personal consciousness to the direction of the Universal Mind. That submission is foreshadowed even in the picture of the Magician, who derives all his power from above. Until we know that of ourselves we can do nothing, we shall never attain to adeptship. The greater the adept, the more complete his personal self-surrender.

Paradoxically, this total submission of the personal life to Life Itself makes us intensely positive in relation to other persons, and in relation to the conditions of our environment. Nobody who follows this course ever becomes a human door-mat. Consciousness of the support of something transcending mere personal human power always results in positive mental attitudes. In the face of some of the appearances confronting us as we go through life, we need something more than just "our" personal energies to carry us through. In order to have courage and persistence in spite of seeming disappointments and difficulties we must know ourselves to be vehicles of a power to which nothing can be an insurmountable obstacle.

The mental attitude suggested by the Hanged Man, then, is "Not my will, but thine." This is ever the position of the adept, as, indeed, it is the position of every person who works in any field of applied science. It is an attitude born of the knowledge that "my will" is an illusive, personal thing which is but the reflection, or mask, of "Thy Will," the real Will, which is the purpose or motive of the cosmic Life—a Will absolutely free, and certain to be realized.

This thought does not imply that the Universal Will visits affliction, disease and poverty upon us. It does not mean that we must be resigned to our troubles, like dumb beasts, making no complaint when they are beaten. It means that in spite of appearances the cosmic Will works always toward good, that the universal Will-to-good cannot possibly be defeated. It means that personality is known for what it is, a partial expression of the All, and that in consequence our personal notions of what is best for us may often be mistaken. Our notions of the ways in which good is coming to us frequently fall short of being adequate anticipations of the blessings ahead. Thus, so long as we continue to make false interpretations, the inexorable laws of the cosmos work out those interpretations in pain-bringing forms.

Yet pain itself is friendly, because it is educative. Suffering, poverty, disease, inharmony and death all have their lessons for us. These are the goads that prod the race onward in its search for truth. We do not fully understand why this is the method, but we can see that the very fact of manifested existence necessitates temporary limitations, with suffering as an inevitable consequence of such limitations. One does not need to be a philosopher to know that civilization is the result of human reaction against pain, the consequence of the human quest for ways to overcome limitation. Disease teaches us the laws of health, frictions in human relationships goad us into the discovery of the secret of harmony, and the wise declare that in the mystery of death lies hidden the secret of immortality.

Thoughts like these are the exact reverse of what most persons think. Practices in mind-control and body-direction such as are taught by psychologists and occultists are laughed at by the world, and people who take them seriously are jeered at as men upside-down. Yet the world's ridicule should be the best evidence that the occultists are right. For the world is sick unto death, writhing in pain, hag-ridden by war, pestilence and famine; but the wise have found the way of health, of happiness and peace.

DEATH

13   **DEATH**   ⅂

XVII

KEY 13: DEATH (NUN)

Nun (N, value 50; as a final letter, 700) is pronounced "noon," and as a noun means "fish." As a verb, because fish are unusually prolific, it means "to sprout, to grow." The essential idea is fertility, fecundity, productiveness, generative power, and these ideas are bound up in thought and language with such words as cause, origin, source, mainspring, groundwork, leaven, and the like.

Motion is the function attributed by Qabalists to Nun, and the Hebrew word for it has the primary meaning of "to walk." From this are derived a great variety of other meanings such as to travel, to grow, to depart, to pass away, to whirl, to sail away, and so on. All motion is change, transformation, modification, variation. Thus, by linking up these ideas with the thought of foundation or groundwork implied by the meanings of the letter Nun, we arrive at the conception that change is the basis of manifestation.

South-West is the direction assigned to Nun in *The Book of Formation*. On the Cube of Space this is the vertical line at the right of the western face of the cube. It is the line uniting the western and southern faces. In relation to Tarot, the direction West is assigned to Key 10, The Wheel of Fortune, and South is the direction corresponding to Key 19, The Sun. West relates also to the planet Jupiter, which governs all rotation and circular movement. The river in Key 13 is a symbol of this, for any river is part of the cycle of transformations affecting the element of water, which rises from the sea to become clouds, descends as rain, and then flows back to the sea through various watercourses. South relates to the Sun, and in the background of Key 13 a rising sun is shown.

Scorpio, a fixed, watery sign, is assigned to Nun. Scorpio is ruled by Mars (Key 16, The Tower), and is said by modern astrologers to be the sign of exaltation of Uranus (Key 0, The Fool). Scorpio governs the sex-organs, and is therefore closely associated with reproduction. It is, moreover, connected with the eighth house of the horoscope, which is called the house of death. Thus this sign is directly connected with the title of Key 13. The corresponding color is blue-green. The musical tone is G-natural.

Imaginative Intelligence is the mode of consciousness attributed to the letter Nun. Qabalists say: "It is the ground of similarity in the likeness of beings." That is, it is the basis of the resemblances which are transmitted through the reproductive function. The choice of the adjective "imaginative" is in accordance with the doctrine of Ageless Wisdom that causation is mental. All changes are primarily changes in mental imagery. Change the image, and ultimately the external form will change.

Death, the title, is, as we have said, obviously related to the astrological meaning of Nun. The Bible says death is the last enemy to be overcome. But how? "Overcome evil with good. Love your enemies." In these two brief sentences is the whole secret.

The forces of change which result in physical death are inimical only because we misunderstand and fear them. They are forces connected with reproduction, and by right use of imagination they may be tamed and transformed, so that they can be utilized for indefinite prolongation of physical existence. Death, like every other event in human life, is a manifestation of law. When we understand the law we can direct the forces of change so as to overcome death. Yet understanding never will be ours until fear, not only of dying, but of death itself, has been overcome by right knowledge, and by right interpretation of the phenomena of physical dissolution.

The symbolism in the Rider pack is Dr. Waite's personal variation from the older versions. Good in some respects, it has one major defect. Before the skeleton rider on the pale horse, among the figures about to fall, is a prelate, wearing a fish-head mitre. This is a reference to the religious dispensation peculiar to the Piscean Age. As this passes away, so will pass away also the notions as to the status of women and children characteristic of the Piscean Age.

This is perfectly true, but Tarot was not invented for the Piscean Age only, and to limit the operation of the law pictured by Key 13 to this one period of human history is to obscure the fact that Key 13 symbolizes something which is at work in every age.

The B.O.T.A version, like that shown in older packs, shows a skeleton with a scythe, reaping living hands, feet and heads, which protrude from the ground. Behind him is a river, and in the background a rising sun. The river moves from north-west to south-east, and the reaper walks in the same direction. One of the heads is male, and wears a crown, the other female and uncrowned. On the south side of the picture is a bush bearing a single white rose. The sky in the background is red.

The skeleton is the basis, or essential thing, in all movements of the human body. Similarly, change or transformation — particularly the transformations connected with reproduction — is the framework which supports the whole body of phenomenal existence. Thus Dr. Waite says: "The veil or mask of life is perpetuated in change, transformation and passage from lower to higher." Note his use of the verb "perpetuated." The letter-name Nun, as a proper noun, as when we read that Joshua was the son of Nun, signifies "perpetuity." In this connection, note that Joshua, Moses' successor, was the great hero of Israel, after whom Jesus was named. There is, moreover, an underlying correspondence between the proper name Nun and the name Joseph. For Nun has growth and development for its basic meaning, and Joseph signifies *multiplication*. Hence, in Jacob's blessing, recorded in the forty-ninth chapter of Genesis, we read: "Joseph is a fruitful bough, even a fruitful bough by a well; whose branches run over the wall."

The name Joshua means literally, "Jah liberates." The divine name Jah is used in the passage from the sixty-eighth Psalm which runs: "Sing unto God, sing praises to his name: extol him that rideth upon the heavens by his name JAH, and rejoice before him." Qabalists ascribe this divine name to Chokmah, or Wisdom, the second aspect of Deity. Chokmah, they say, is also the Sphere of the Zodiac, or Masloth, "the highways of the stars." He that "rideth upon the heavens" is the Divine Wisdom which finds expression in the astronomical order of which our solar system is but a small part. Consequently, Joshua or "Jah liberates," really means that the entire cosmic order is fundamentally liberative. It has an irresistible tendency toward the manifestation of freedom.

In the human heart, this tendency is a continual urge. It is the basic motivation of every normal person. We hunger and thirst for liberty. For freedom we sacrifice everything else; and if we are ignorant, we believe we can attain freedom for ourselves by enslaving others. Yet the ignorant and the wise are basically the same, because the realization of perfect freedom is the common ideal of all men.

To what we adopt as an ideal, to that we give homage. It is the object of our worship. To it we bow the knee. Thus, when it is written, "At the name of Jesus every knee shall bow," we should not suppose it to be a prophecy of a time when all men will be nominal, exoteric Christians. The name Jesus is just another way of saying the name Joshua, and to the ideal of human liberty indicated by the fundamental meaning of that name, to the wisdom which declares the whole cosmic order to be a process making for freedom, every heart responds.

What Ageless Wisdom always has declared is that everything works together for freedom and for good, to them that love God. Modern science begins to confirm this ancient intuition by showing us that no force or law of the universe is inimical to man, or an obstacle to his freedom. To love God is not to go into silly ecstasies of emotional adoration for a personal Deity. Love is the fruit of understanding; and when we understand that the One Life which finds expression in the order of the heavens of which our world-system is a part is a Life working always toward the liberation of mankind, we advance from the fear of the Lord which is only the beginning of wisdom into the recognition of the perfect beauty of the order of which we are a part. This perfect love casts out fear, and with the coming of this deeper understanding comes freedom from fear of death.

It is by death that social changes for the better come to pass. Old ideas pass away with the death of the persons who hold them. New ideas gain currency as the new generation comes to maturity. Thus the actual fact of death is an instrument of progress. And now the time is close at hand when man shall master the secret of death itself.

Psychologically, the emphasis falls on imagination. Change your ideas and your old conception of personality dies. Every few years you have a new body, made up of trillions of tiny beings, or cells. Change your intellectual patterns, and with the passing away of the present generation of cells new ones will come to take their places. In the mental nucleus of each tiny cell, implanted there by subconscious response to your new patterns, will be an impulse to realize the new thought in body-structure, in function, and in external action.

If your pattern be built in accordance with the ideas developed through the Tarot series, and culminating in the self-surrender pictured by the Hanged Man, it will lead to a complete transformation of your personality. The "old man" dies. One who arrives at this state can say with St. Paul, "I die daily." Every morning becomes a resurrection to the awakened soul. All the old motives, all the petty

ambitions, all the foolish opinions and prejudices gradual-
ly die out, as the cells which carry them are eliminated in
the ordinary course of body-repair.

Thus, little by little, there comes a complete readjust-
ment of one's personal conceptions of life and its values.
The change from the personal to the universal viewpoint
is so radical that mystics often compare it to death. They
are more literal than many of their readers suppose. It is by
the death and reproduction of body-cells that patterns
created by imagination are finally fixed in personal consciousness. Then it is that we may truly declare, "The
Kingdom of Spirit is embodied in my flesh."

TEMPERANCE

14 TEMPERANCE

XVIII

KEY 14: TEMPERANCE (SAMEKH)

Samekh (soft C, or S, value 60) means "tent-peg," or "prop." It is what makes a tent secure, and thus corresponds to what would now be suggested to us by the foundation of a house. It is therefore the letter-symbol of that which is the basis or support of our house of life. It is that which sustains, preserves and maintains our personal existence.

Wrath is the quality associated with Samekh, but this is a blind. The literal meaning of the original Hebrew noun is "quivering" or "vibration." A similar blind is found in the use of the Green noun thumos, also translated "wrath" in the New Testament. The Hebrew word is RVGZ, and its number is 216, the value of RAIH, sight, the function attributed to Key 4, The Emperor. 216 is also the value of ARIH, lion, the name of the zodiacal sign associated with the Tarot picture of Strength, and the value of GBVRH, Geburah, Severity, the name of the strength aspect of the number 5.

The numerical correspondence of these Hebrew words indicates a basic identity of meaning. Vibration is the fundamental nature of the fiery power which makes sight possible, and that same power is the source of all our strength.

Furthermore, when translated into Tarot pictures, the word RVGZ becomes this sequence: The Sun; the Hierophant; the High Priestess; the Lovers. Lay these Keys on a table, and study them. You will get intimations as to the real meaning of the vibratory force which would otherwise escape you. Note that the first letter corresponds to the sun, the second to the sign Taurus, ruled by Venus, the third to the moon, and the last to Gemini, ruled by Mercury. Add the numbers of these Tarot trumps. The result is

153

32. As there is no Tarot Key bearing this number, add the digits, and the result, 5, is the number of the Hierophant. This, too, is the number resulting from the reduction of 14, the number of Temperance.

The idea is that vibration is the basis of manifestation, and that all vibration is essentially like sound, the mode of vibration which is particularly associated with the Hierophant. Vibration is fluctuating motion, undulation, pulsation, alternation. It takes wave-forms.

West-Above, the direction assigned to Samekh, corresponds to the upper boundary of the western face of the Cube of Space. This is the line of junction between West (Key 10, The Wheel of Fortune) and Above (Key 1, The Magician). Here is indicated the combination of the idea of cycles and rotation with that of concentration and attentive observation of experience. We shall find this developed in the picture of Temperance.

Sagittarius, the Archer, is a fiery, common sign, ruled by Jupiter (Key 10, The Wheel of Fortune). It governs the thighs and hips, which support the weight of the body in standing and sitting. The color-correspondence is blue. The musical tone is G-sharp or A-flat.

Tentative Intelligence, or *Intelligence of Probation or Trial*, indicates a mode of consciousness wherein experience becomes the test of ideas. It is the kind of consciousness which puts theory to the test of practical application, which makes experiments to verify hypotheses, which does laboratory work. All such work consists in the examination and modification of various modes of vibration.

Temperance, in the day when Tarot was invented, meant "tempering" or "modifying." It therefore suggests adaptation. (Here note that the digit value of 14 is 5, and 5 means adaptation.) Adaptation is the basis of all practical work in Hermetic science. *The Emerald Tablet* says: "As all things are from One, so all have their birth from this One thing by adaptation." Hermetic scientists endeavor to imitate nature, and adaptation is their method. To adapt is to equalize, to adjust, to co-ordinate, to equilibrate. Therefore it is written: "Equilibrium is the basis of the Great Work."

Over the head of the angel, in the B.O.T.A. version of Key 14, is a rainbow. This is a direct reference to Sagittarius, because the Hebrew name for this sign is QShTh, Qesheth, the Bow. This is also the "bow of promise." In the Rider pack, Dr. Waite, with characteristic fondness for being mysterious, substituted for the rainbow iris flowers, in reference to Iris, Greek goddess of the rainbow. Behind this rainbow symbolism are recondite Qabalistic meanings upon which it would be unprofitable to enlarge in this elementary text. Take what is written here as a signpost. If you wish to go further, consider its meaning. You might also look up Iris in a good dictionary of mythology.

At the bottom of the picture is a pool, corresponding to the ninth Hebrew Sephirah, Yesod, which is the seat of the automatic consciousness, or vital soul, in man. On the Tree of Life, the path corresponding to Key 14 connects the sixth Sephirah, Tiphareth, at the center of the Tree, to Yesod, and thus the pool at the bottom of the picture is an occult reference to what Qabalists have in mind when they call Yesod the Sphere of the Moon.

The path rising from the pool appears again in Key 18, and will be more fully explained in connection with that card. Observe that it rises over rolling ground, and thus imitates the wave-motion which is characteristic of all forms of vibration.

At the upper end of the path is a crown. It signifies attainment, mastery, and like ideas. It has also a reference to the esoteric meanings of the number 1, which Qabalists call "The Crown." The end of the path of attainment is the realization of the crown of perfect union with the Primal Will. The twin peaks on either side of the path, under the crown, are Wisdom, the second Sephirah, and Understanding, the third.

The Tarot

The angel is Michael, archangel of fire, angel of the sun, and ruler of the South (Key 19, The Sun). Michael is also specially connected with Tiphareth on the Tree of Life. The solar symbol on his head establishes his identity, as does his yellow hair, and the rays streaming from it. The fact that Sagittarius is a fiery sign carries the correspondence still further. So do the fiery wings of the angel.

His white robe represents purity and wisdom. At the neck are written, in Hebrew characters, the letters of the Tetragrammaton, IHVH. Below the letters is a golden star with seven points. This has special reference to skill, because to make such a star, a circle must be divided into seven equal parts. There is no exact mathematical formula for this. Thus the division must be made by trial and error. Here we have the underlying idea of the Intelligence of Probation or Trial. The seven points of the star symbolize the seven Spirits of God, or aspects of the Divine Life. They correspond also to the seven sacred planets, the seven alchemical metals, and the seven chakras of the Yogis.

One foot of the angel rests on water, symbol of the cosmic mind-stuff. The other is on land, symbol of concrete physical manifestation.

In the Rider pack, the angel pours water from the cup in his left hand to that in his right. The cups are of gold, to symbolize the idea that all forms of life-expression have radiant energy for their basic substance. The upper cup is self-consciousness, corresponding to the man in Key 6, The Lovers. The other cup is subconsciousness, corresponding to the woman in the same picture. The stream of water (mind-stuff) vibrates between them. Furthermore, actions and reaction are intimated, for when the lower cup is filled he will reverse the position of the cups, and that which is now above will become that which is below.

In the B.O.T.A. version, the symbolism is slightly different, and is based on the esoteric Tarot which has never been published in its entirety. The angel stands between a

156

lion and an eagle. The lion is, in the colored Keys, a dark,
earthy brown, like the body of the Devil in Key 15, because
he is a symbol of that same devil, in the guise of a lion,
seeking whom he may devour. Yet this is also a symbol of
fire, and because ARIH, Arieh, the Lion, has the same
numeration as GBVRH, Geburah, Strength, the lion is a
symbol for the Mars-force concentrated in Geburah. This
force is exalted in the sign Capricorn, and when the Tarot
is placed on the Tree of Life, Key 14 stands between the
paths of Capricorn and Scorpio. Thus the composition of
this version of Key 14 is a reference to the place of the Key
on the Tree of Life. For the eagle on the other side of the
picture is a symbol for the watery sign Scorpio.

Upon the fiery lion the angel pours water. From the
torch in his left hand five flames, shaped like the letter
Yod, fall on the head of the eagle, and a sixth flame rises.
Water on fire, and fire on water, or the action and reaction
of opposites, is thus shown; and this carries out the
general idea of tempering or modifying indicated by the
title of the Key.

The angel is the real I AM, or Ego of the entire human
race, having its seat in Tiphareth, the sixth Sephirah.
He is shown adapting and modifying the personal stream
of psychic energy in the actions and reactions of the
self-conscious and subconscious aspects of human
personality.

The practical import of the picture is this: We do
nothing of ourselves. The Holy Guardian Angel makes all
the tests and trials which lead us along the path of attainment. Know this, but act as if you were making the tests
yourself. The only correction necessary is the intellectual
correction. For practical purposes, the wise man acts just
as if he were doing things "on his own." He *knows* better,
that's all.

In your practice, shoot at some definite mark. Quit
accepting theories and statements — no matter how
plausible they may be — until you have tested them out in

actual practice. The purpose of Ageless Wisdom is to get you to try, not to persuade you to accept. Thus it is written, "The only failure is failure to try." By trial you will soon realize that the real working power which makes the experiments is something higher than your personality. It is the Angel, on whose robe is written the identifying name of That which was, and is, and shall be.

Finally, all your experiments will be in equalization, in the co-ordination of vibratory activities. There is nothing in the cosmos but vibration, and all forms of vibration may be modified and managed by mental control.

THE DEVIL

15 THE DEVIL ל

XIX

KEY 15: THE DEVIL (AYIN)

Ayin (O, value 70) means "eye" and "foundation." It signifies also the external, superficial appearances of things. As the organ of sight, the eye is the most important sense-tool, hence symbolists take it to represent all sensation, just as the lion, king of beasts, is taken as the representative of all subhuman modes of life-expression. The eye is an orb; vision is limited by the circle of the horizon; through the eye we see appearances only. Hence the eye represents the limitations of the visible, and the bondage of ignorance resulting from the acceptance of these limitations and appearances as being all there is.

Mirth, the function of consciousness attributed by Qabalists to the letter Ayin, is usually provoked by incongruity, by human weaknesses, foibles, and shortcomings. Nevertheless, laughter is prophylactic. It purifies subconsciousness and dissolves mental complexes and conflicts. In a hymn to the sun-god Ra we read: "Thy priests go forth at dawn, they wash their hearts with laughter." This is a prescription we may all follow to advantage.

West-Below, the direction assigned to Ayin, combines West (Key 10, The Wheel of Fortune) with Below (Key 2, The High Priestess). Here is an intimation that whatever is denoted by Key 15 is the result of impressions made by the apparently mechanical, fatal revolutions of circumstance (The Wheel of Fortune) upon human subconsciousness (High Priestess). On the Cube of Space, the line West-Below connects the lower end of the line North-West to the lower end of the line South-West, and is the lower boundary of the western face of the cube, or the western boundary of the lower face.

Capricorn, the Goat, is a cardinal, earthy sign, governing the knees, to which we are brought in prayer by our sense of bondage and personal insufficiency. The natives of Capricorn are said to be quiet, studious, and somewhat inclined to materialism. Saturn (Key 21, The World) rules Capricorn, and Mars (Key 16, The Tower) is exalted therein. The color-correspondence is blue-violet or indigo. The musical tone is A-natural.

Renewing Intelligence is the mode of consciousness attributed to Ayin. This is directly related to Mirth, because the perception of incongruities is what actually brings forth new ideas and adaptations. An incongruity is something which does not fit. When we find a fact that does not fit in with our beliefs, we are obliged to revise our theories, unless we are the sort of "green apple" who prefers a comfortable lie to an uncomfortable truth.

It has been, indeed, the incongruity between man's apparent bondage to circumstance and his ineradicable intuition that somehow or other he is intended to rule nature which has driven the race forward in those avenues of research which lead to freedom.

Internally, we know that we are potential lords of creation. But here we meet a check, and there a defeat, and so we try to explain why we are not actually as free as we feel ourselves internally to be. The symbolism of Key 15 represents the cruder forms of man's answers to the question, "What keeps me from expressing this inner freedom I feel?" At the same time, this picture indicates the correct solution to the problem, and points to the way which leads out of the difficulty.

The Devil is the English for the Latin *diabolus*, adversary. The picture refers to man's ideas concerning the nature of that which seems so relentlessly to oppose his struggles for freedom. In commenting on this, let us once more remind you of the words ascribed to Jehovah in Isaiah 45. Remember, too, that the Devil personifies the serpent-power represented by the letter Teth and Key 8, Strength.

Key 15: The Devil (Ayin)

The name for the serpent which tempted Eve is NChSh, Nachash, and the number of this word is 358, the value of MShICh, Messiah. Here is a profound subtlety, for numerical identity between Hebrew words points to some inner correspondence of meaning. Finally, it has been said: "The Devil is God, as He is misunderstood by the wicked."

The number of the trump is 15, which is the number of IH, Jah, the divine name especially ascribed to Wisdom. The same number is shown by the number of trefoils on the tiara of the Hierophant. By addition of digits, 15 reduces to 6, the number of the Lovers. Furthermore, 15 is the sum of the numbers from 0 through 5, so that the Hierophant (5), regarded as the summation of a series beginning with 0, refers also to Key 15. Compare, now, the Devil with the Lovers and the Hierophant.

The background of Key 15 is black, color of darkness, ignorance, limitation, and also of that which is hidden or occult. Here is an intimation that ignorance is the underlying cause of bondage. A hint, also, that the ridiculous figure of the Devil is a veil for a profound secret of practical occultism.

The Devil himself is the polar opposite of the angel shown in the preceding major trump. He is also a caricature of the angel over the heads of the Lovers, even as the figures below him are bestialized reproductions of the man and the woman in Key 6.

Goat's horns on his head refer to the sign Capricorn. His wings are bat's wings, signifying the powers of darkness. His face is that of a goat, but he has the ears of a donkey, to suggest the obstinacy and stubbornness of materialism. His body is thickset and gross, and of an earthen color, to represent the earthy quality of the sign Capricorn. One side is masculine, the other feminine, because what he represents partakes of the characteristics of both sexes.

Between his horns is a white, inverted Pentagram. This is a key to the whole meaning of the figure. For the Penta-

163

gram is the symbol of man, and an inverted Pentagram suggests the reversal of true understanding of man's place in the cosmos. In point of fact, the mistaken estimate of man's powers and possibilities is all that keeps anyone in bondage.

The Devil's uplifted right hand has all its fingers open, as if in contradiction to the sign of esotericism made by the Hierophant. The latter's gesture says: "What you see is not all there is to know." The Devil's gesture intimates: "What sensation reports is all there is to it." On the palm of this uplifted hand is outlined an astrological symbol of the planet Saturn, ruling in Capricorn. Saturn is the planet of limitation, inertia, and therefore of ignorance.

In his left hand is a torch, burning wastefully, and giving little light. The torch is a phallic symbol, representing the transmission of life from generation to generation. Its fiery quality refers also to the exaltation of the Mars vibration in Capricorn. In one sense, this is the fiery torch of revolution, based on materialistic interpretations of experience, the torch of terrorism and anarchy.

It may be worth mentioning that this Devil has a navel. He is a human product, begotten of man's ignorance. A symbol of Mercury is shown just below his navel, to indicate that he is a product of faulty observation and superficial reasoning.

His feet are the claws of an eagle. The eagle is the bird corresponding to the sign Scorpio. Here the eagle's claws refer to the materialization and misuse of the reproductive power, and its debasement in the service of sensuality.

The Devil sits on a pedestal which is a half-cube. Since a cube represents That which was, is, and shall be, a half-cube symbolizes half-knowledge of that reality. Half-knowledge perceives nothing but the visible, sensory side of existence.

To this half-cube are chained smaller figures, representing self-conscious and subconscious modes of human mentality. Their horns, hoofs and tails show that when reasoning takes its premises from surface appearances, human consciousness becomes bestialized. Observe that, though they are chained to the cube, the loops of the chains are so large that they might lift them off their heads. Their bondage is imaginary.

This picture represents the first stage of spiritual unfoldment. It is the stage of conscious bondage. The Devil personifies the false conception that man is bound by material conditions, the false notion that he is a slave to necessity, a sport of chance.

In truth, the forces which appear to be our adversaries are always ready to serve us. The one condition is that we understand our essential freedom, and take account of the hidden side of existence. Then, when we conform our practice to our knowledge, liberation begins. The Devil is sensation, divorced by ignorance from understanding. Yet he is also what brings renewal, because we can make no real effort to be free until we feel our limitations. Until they irk us, we can make no effort to strike off our chains.

THE TOWER

16   THE TOWER

XX

KEY 16: The Tower (Peh)

Peh (P, Ph, F; value 80; as a final letter, 800) means "the mouth as the organ of speech." It therefore symbolizes power of utterance. Out of it are the issues of life.

North, the direction assigned to Peh, is the place of darkness, of the unknown, of the sun's annual death. On the Cube of Space, as ordinarily shown in diagrams, it is the side on the observer's left.

Mars, the planet attributed to Peh, rules Aries (Key 4, The Emperor) and Scorpio (Key 13, Death), and is exalted in Capricorn (Key 15, The Devil). According to astrologers, the Mars vibration is scientific, and is active in sight. It is the force which finds expression in reproduction, and it gives tonicity to the muscles, being thus the basis of all human activity. In its psychological manifestations it is the destructive, iconoclastic force which tears down the structures of ancient custom and tradition. Its color is scarlet, and the corresponding musical tone is C-natural.

Grace and Sin, or Beauty and Ugliness, are the pair of opposites attributed by Qabalists to the letter Peh, because the issues of life, directed by human speech, result in one or the other. Sin, or "missing the mark," results in maladjustment and ugliness. Hitting the mark in right action results in the manifestation of beauty.

Active or Exciting Intelligence is the mode of consciousness attributed to Peh. It stirs up activity, sets things going, produces changes, effects transformations. Note, in this connection, that in Key 1 the Magician wears a red outer garment.

The Tower is one of several titles, among them being "The Lightning-struck Tower," "The Fire of Heaven," and "The House of God." It refers traditionally to the Tower of

Babel, at which human speech was confounded. When this Key is called "La Maison de Dieu," or "The House of God," the title indicates the exoteric structure of religious belief. Note that the number of this Key, 16, digits to 7, the number of the Chariot, which refers to Speech.

The lightning is a masculine symbol. In the Bhagavad-Gita, Krishna says: "Among weapons, I am the thunder-bolt." It is interesting to note that when lightning-flashes, artificially produced, were photographed at the Westinghouse laboratories, they were shown to be spirals, rather than zig-zags. This fact may have been known to the ancients, for *The Chaldean Oracles of Zoroaster* speak of the Supreme Spirit as "the god who energizes a spiral force." In olden times lightning was an emblem of fecundation and nutrition, as we learn from Plutarch, who says: "The agriculturalists call the lightning the fertilizer of the waters, and so regard it."

The lightning-flash is the power drawn from above by the Magician. It is the sword of the Charioteer, the scepter of the Emperor, the force which turns the Wheel of Fortune, the scythe of Death, and the light streaming from the Hermit's lantern. It breaks down existing forms in order to make room for new ones.

For Qabalists, the lightning-flash is a symbol of the ten-fold emanation of the Life-power. In the B.O.T.A. version of Key 16, therefore, the thunderbolt is so drawn that it corresponds to the familiar Qabalistic diagram of the Tree of Life. Concerning this *The Book of Formation* says: "Ten ineffable Sephiroth (numerations); their appearance is like that of a flash of lightning, their goal is infinite." In terms of consciousness, the lightning-flash symbolizes a sudden, momentary glimpse of truth, a flash of inspiration which breaks down structures of ignorance and false reasoning.

The tower has the same basic meaning as the garden of the Magician, the throne of the Emperor, the turning Wheel, the field in Key 13. It is subconsciousness, considered as the root-substance which takes form, first as mental images, and ultimately as physical things. From moment to moment, throughout all time, it is being transformed. It is the Prakriti of the Hindus, concerning which it is written: "True knowledge makes Prakriti disappear, first as containing Purusha (the I AM), and then as separate from Purusha."

The falling figures correspond to the chained prisoners in the preceding picture. They fall headfirst, because the sudden influx of spiritual consciousness represented by the lightning-flash completely upsets all our old notions about the relations between subconsciousness and self-consciousness.

These figures are clothed, and the man wears both red and blue, to show a mixture of self-conscious and subconscious activities. Similarly, the woman is shod with red, but wears a blue robe. The woman, furthermore, is crowned. In false knowledge, subconscious motives are permitted to dominate the personality. Thus people excuse themselves for unintelligent action by saying, "I can't help it; that's the way I feel."

This domination of personality by emotion, and by telepathic invasion through subconsciousness, is overcome by right knowledge. So is the concealment and division between self-consciousness and subconsciousness, here indicated by the fact that the falling figures are fully clothed.

The crown knocked from the tower by the lightning-flash is the materialistic notion that matter and form are the ruling principles of existence. Since "Crown" is a Qabalistic term relating to the number 1, and to Will, this crown refers to the false monism of the materialist, and to the false interpretation of will which makes it something personal, something which may be set against the impulse originating in the cosmic Purpose.

The tower has twenty-two courses of masonry, and is built of brick. In Hebrew, the word for moon and the word for brick is spelt with precisely the same letters, LBNH, because the white Babylonian bricks resemble moonlight. Bricks are made of clay, and clay is the symbol of Adam. Thus the tower suggests a structure of human speech, because its twenty-two courses correspond to the number of letters in the Hebrew alphabet. It is reared on a lonely peak, and suggests the fallacy of personal isolation which is the basis of all false philosophy.

By contrast with the twenty-two courses of masonry, twenty-two Hebrew Yods are shown, hanging in the air on either side of the building. These represent the twenty-two letters of the Hebrew alphabet, and the forces corresponding thereto. Ten, on one side of the Tower are arranged in the form of the Tree of Life. They also represent the elementary and planetary letters. The twelve on the other side represent the twelve zodiacal letters. They hang in the air, to indicate that the forces they symbolize rest on no physical foundation.

This picture corresponds to the second stage of spiritual unfoldment, wherein a series of sudden, fitful inspirations leads to the perception that the structure of knowledge built on the foundation of the fallacy of personal separateness is a tower of false science. At this stage, the advancing seeker for wisdom suffers the destruction of his whole former philosophy. For this tower is built upon a foundation of misapprehension. The whole structure is an elaboration of superficial observation, traditional race-thought, false reasoning and an erroneous theory of will.

THE STAR

17   **THE STAR**

XXI

KEY 17: THE STAR (TZADDI)

Tzaddi (Ts, Tz, or Cz as in "Czar"; value 90, as a final letter, 900) means "fish-hook," signifying that which draws the fish (Nun) out of the water (Mem). The water is reflected, personal existence, symbolized by the Hanged Man. It is also, in a sense, the ocean of subconscious mentality. The fish symbolizes transforming and reproductive power. The activity which lifts the fish up out of the material relations of personal existence, and utilizes the reproductive forces as a regenerative agency, is what is indicated here.

Now, a fish-hook is a symbol of angling. Thus in our thought it is related to the ideas of experimentation, quest and research. It is a quest for that which is not definitely realized as yet, a sort of groping, a feeling of one's way, that we speak of as "fishing." What is clearly intimated here is that whatever the fish-hook symbolizes must be some agency or instrumentality whereby one investigates the unseen and the unknown, whereby one makes attempts to solve enigmas, or to discover secrets, or to follow a more or less faint trail leading to the solution of a mystery.

Meditation is the function attributed to Tzaddi. It has been defined as "an unbroken flow of knowledge in a particular object." It is a fishing for truth in the depths of subconsciousness. The Hebrew word means literally "conception," and is a transference to things mental of the idea of physical conception. It refers to the budding or germination of ideas. Germinal processes in both plant and animal organisms go on in darkness. They are, moreover, rudimentary. What we are considering here, therefore, has to do with the early stages of mental unfoldment, with the genesis of ideas, rather than with their full development.

Practically, meditation is the only safe regenerative method, because it draws nerve-force up from the reproductive centers without any actual fixation of attention on the centers themselves, and without any thought about the sex-functions.

South-Above, the direction attributed to Tzaddi, is the line on the Cube of Space joining the upper ends of the lines South-West and South-East, and forming the southern boundary of the upper face of the cube, or the upper boundary of the southern face. It combines South (Key 19, The Sun) with Above (Key 1, The Magician). This is the combination of the radiant energy of the sun with the directive influence of Mercury. Meditation is the direction of currents of solar force by acts of self-conscious attention.

Aquarius, the Water-bearer, an airy, fixed sign, is attributed by Qabalists to Tzaddi. It is represented by the Man among the "living creatures" of Ezekiel and the Apocalypse. Its astrological symbol is shown on the Wheel of Fortune, two wavy lines, one above the other. This is also an alchemical symbol for dissolution, and we have already seen that *solution* is one of the ideas connected with the symbol of the fish-hook. The Aquarius symbol, moreover, is one of many Hermetic representations of the axiom, "That which is above is as that which is below."

Ancient astrology made Saturn (Key 21, The World) ruler of Aquarius. Modern astrologers find that this sign receives also the influence of Uranus (Key 0, The Fool). Aquarius governs the ankles. Aquarians are said to be intuitive, and fond of occult research. They succeed in pursuits where steady mental application and intense concentration are necessary. That is, they are naturally meditative, naturally given to activities which lead to the discovery of difficult, elusive modes of truth. All this agrees with the ideas associated with Tzaddi. The color-correspondence to Aquarius is violet. Its musical tone is A-sharp or B-flat.

Natural Intelligence is the mode of consciousness attributed to Tzaddi. The Hebrew of the adjective "natural" is from the root TBO, meaning literally "to sink." The connection with the fish-hook, which must be dropped in water to catch the fish, is obvious. Natural Intelligence, or awareness of the hidden qualities of nature, is arrived at by meditation. This is the great secret of the occult power wielded by Oriental adepts. See Patanjali's *Yoga Aphorisms*, for the enumeration of the many "powers" which may be developed by intense concentration and prolonged meditation.

Because the number 17 reduces to 8, this picture has occult correspondence to the trump entitled Strength. It shows the method whereby knowledge of the Great Secret is attained. This method solves the mysteries of nature, and, as the picture shows, unveils her to the enlightened seer.

The great yellow star signifies the cosmic radiant energy which is sent forth from the various suns and fixed stars of the universe. It has eight points. Thus its geometrical construction is like that of the Wheel of Fortune, or the symbols of Spirit embroidered on the dress of the Fool. This star symbolizes the solar energy hinted at by the attribution of the direction South-Above to the letter Tzaddi. The inventors of Tarot used innumerable devices to remind us that in our mental and magical work we are using an actual force which has definite physical forms of expression. Meditation modifies and transmutes the personal expression of this cosmic energy, and that personal expression is what we term nerve-force.

The seven smaller stars refer to the seven "interior stars," which are the same as the "chakras" mentioned by Hindu occultists. They are also the "metals" of alchemy, and the planets of esoteric astrology. They are: Sacral plexus, Saturn, Lead, Muladhara chakra; Prostatic ganglion (below the navel), Mars, Iron, Svadistthana chakra; Solar Plexus, Jupiter, Tin, Manipura chakra; Cardiac plexus,

Sun, Gold, Anahata chakra; Pharyngeal plexus, Venus, Copper or Brass, Visuddhi chakra; Pituitary, or post-nasal ganglion, Moon, Silver, Ajna chakra; Pineal gland, Mercury, Quicksilver, Sahasrara chakra. They are shown white, to indicate purification.

As said, one should beware of fixing attention upon the centers themselves. Their activity may be stimulated by engaging in the kind of meditation suggested by the modes of intelligence attributed to the corresponding letters. Thus Saturn is represented in Tarot by Key 21 and the Administrative Intelligence; Mars by Key 16 and the Exciting Intelligence; Jupiter by Key 10 and the Intelligence of Conciliation; the Sun by Key 19 and the Collective Intelligence; Venus by Key 3 and the Luminous Intelligence; the Moon by Key 2 and the Uniting Intelligence; Mercury by Key 1 and the Intelligence of Transparency.

Using the Tarot Keys just enumerated as centers for concentration will arouse the activity of the corresponding centers, without any danger of physical congestion. Remember, this is mental angling. This outline and its explanations are only guide-posts. They are intended to tell you how to make use of Tarot. Yet further investigation and study must supplement what you will find in these pages. When Eliphas Levi promises the acquisition of a universal science from the Tarot, he implies that the student must use the Keys. You have just now been referred to Patanjali's *Yoga Aphorisms*, and their enumeration of the powers to be gained from meditation. The Tarot pictures are keys to the liberation of such powers by the same method. Behind their symbols are practical secrets of occultism which cannot be put into words.

Lesser secrets, too, are hidden there, which might be written out; but my teachers have convinced me that such a course would be inadvisable. The plain truth is that the first rule in occult teaching is that the pupil should be told almost nothing that he can find out for himself. These pages put you on the track of discovery. Your own work with the Tarot Keys is the only thing that will bring you to the point where you will possess actual first-hand knowledge of the secrets of practical occultism.

The mountain in the background means just what it does in Keys 6 and 8. It is a symbol of the Great Work.

The bird on the bush is a scarlet ibis. This is the Egyptian bird sacred to Hermes, the Magician. Its long bill is a natural fish-hook. Perched on a tree which represents the human brain and nervous system, it symbolizes the act of bringing intellectual activity, or the thought process, to rest by concentration. We have to stop thinking in order to meditate properly, and when we stop thinking Truth unveils herself to us.

The woman is Hathor, or Mother Nature. In some respects we may identify her with the Empress. In others she corresponds to the High Priestess. She is also the woman who, in Key 8, tames the lion and opens his mouth. For meditation is largely the utilization and direction of the powers of deduction and imagination peculiar to subconsciousness. The knowledge gained in meditation is gleaned from the imperishable record of the memory of nature, symbolized by the scroll of the High Priestess. Furthermore, meditation develops specific powers, and it does this by controlling the animal forces in human personality, as pictured in Key 8.

The pool is the universal consciousness, or reservoir of cosmic mind-stuff, which is stirred into vibration by the act of meditation. This is indicated by the stream of water flowing into the pool from the right-hand pitcher. It indicates direct modification of the cosmic mind-stuff apart from sensory experience. The stream flowing from the other pitcher divides into five rivulets, which flow back to the pool along the ground. They indicate the fact that meditation also modifies sensation, and unfolds higher and subtler types of sense experience.

The left knee of the woman, supporting her weight, rests on earth. Her right knee, bent to form the angle of a square, is over the pool, and her right foot rests on the surface of the water. Thus the earth supports her weight, but she balances herself by water. That is, sensations derived from physical forms are the main support of meditation, but these are balanced by experience gained direct from subconsciousness.

This picture shows the third stage of spiritual unfoldment. It is the calm which follows the storm depicted by Key 16. It is a period of quest and search. The light is dim, like starlight, but these stars are distant suns. Thus it is written: "When you have found the beginning of the way, the star of your soul will show its light."

THE MOON

18 THE MOON ♇

XXII

KEY 18: THE MOON (QOPH)

Qoph (Q, value 100) means "back of the head." This is the part of the skull which contains the cerebellum and the medulla oblongata. These parts of the brain are related to the functions of human personality which man shares with the rest of the animal kingdom. The medulla, in particular governs some of the most important bodily activities. The cells of this organ remain awake when the rest of the brain is asleep.

"Head," moreover, means "chief," in Hebrew as in English; and in the sequence of the Hebrew alphabet, the letter Qoph, "back of the head," precedes the letter Resh, which means "head, or countenance." Thus, in the series of letters Qoph is actually behind, or back of, Resh, the head. Qoph therefore represents what comes before the dominion and rulership of which the word "head" is a symbol. This is true, also, of the occult meanings of Qoph, which relate to states of consciousness anterior to perfect control, and leading thereto.

Sleep is the function assigned to Qoph. Sleep is the period of physiological repair, during which the cells of the body undergo subtle changes which make the advancing student of occultism ready to experience and understand facts and phenomena concealed from ordinary men. These facts are the experiential basis of Ageless Wisdom.

The word translated "sleep" is from *The Book of Formation*. It is a technical term in Rabbinical Hebrew, spelt ShINH, and having the value 365. Furthermore, by transposition of letters, it may be read HShIN, or Ha-Shin, "the tooth." Thus it is a word whose number, like the Greek *abraxas*, which also adds to 365, may be a mystery-

The Tarot

term relating to the number of days, and to the number of "eons" ruling the year. It also hints at a correspondence to the "Holy Letter," Shin.

South-Below, the direction attributed to Qoph, corresponds to the lower line on the southern face of the Cube of Space. This line connects the lower end of the line South-West to the lower end of the line South-East. It is the line of junction between the southern face of the cube (Key 19) and the lower face (Key 2). One suggestion is that the solar radiance is reflected by subconsciousness. In the processes anterior to complete control, the directive action of cosmic tendencies is reflected into the personal sphere of action by the agency of subconscious states. Up to a certain point, the cosmic Life-power molds its vehicles without their co-operation. Later, those vehicles become aware of what is going on, and share consciously in the work.

Pisces, the Fishes, a mutable, watery sign, is attributed to the letter Qoph. It is ruled by Jupiter (Key 10) and by Neptune (Key 12). Consideration of the Tarot Keys here indicated will make the meaning clearer.

The processes we are now learning about are the direct outcome of the "wheels within wheels" of the interlocking cycles and rotations of cosmic activities. At the same time, there is a point in human evolution, represented by the Hanged Man, at which we become aware of the fact that personality is only an instrument or channel for the universal forces active in the Great Work. This awareness is also part of the developmental process represented by the symbolism of Key 18.

It is also related to the sign Pisces because that sign governs the feet of man; and because feet are the pathmakers, Pisces relates to that Way of which the beginning is found when meditation reveals the "star of the soul." Venus is said to be exalted in Pisces. That is to say, what the Empress symbolizes reaches its highest expression in this sign, and therefore in the process occultly corresponding to it. Thus we may expect to find that imagination plays an important part in the activities now under consideration. The color corresponding to Pisces is violet-red. The musical tone is B-natural.

Corporeal Intelligence means "body consciousness," that is, the aggregate intelligence of the cells of the body. The root of the word translated "corporeal" is a Hebrew verb meaning "to rain upon," and we shall find an indication of this in the symbolism of Key 18.

The number 18 is 9 by reduction. The Hermit is the goal of the path shown in this picture. With him we are united, according to occult teaching, whenever we experience dreamless sleep. Profound sleep is the state in which personal consciousness is perfectly joined to the real I AM.

The Moon symbolizes the reflected light of subconsciousness. The drops of light falling from it correspond to the implication that "corporeal" is related to "rain." They are eighteen Hebrew Yods, corresponding to the number of the Key. (In the Rider pack the number is 15, which somewhat confuses the symbolism.) The number 18 is the value of the Hebrew noun ChI, Chai, signifying "life." Thus the falling Yods refer to the descent of the life-force from above into the conditions of corporeal existence.

The pool below is the same as that shown in the fourteenth and seventeenth Keys. It is the "great deep" of cosmic mind-stuff, out of which emerges the "dry land" of physical manifestation. From it all organic life proceeds. The pool also refers to the ninth of the Qabalistic Sephiroth, Yesod, which is known as the Sphere of the Moon, and is the seat of the Vital Soul, manifested in man as the automatic consciousness, generally referred to in this book as subconsciousness.

The shell-fish climbing from the pool is a symbol of the early stages of conscious unfoldment. In these first developments of consciousness, the individual seems to be isolated from the rest of nature. In a certain aspect of

Tarot, related to Egyptian occult doctrines, the shell-fish symbolizes the god Khephra.

The path, rising and falling, has been worn by the feet (Pisces) of those who have traveled this way before. It passes between two animals of the same genus, both canine. One, a wolf, remains what nature made him. The other, a dog, is a product of human adaptation. Thus the path passes between the extremes of nature and art.

At its very beginning, where it rises from the margin of the pool, the path is bordered by stones and plants, symbols of the mineral and vegetable kingdoms. Then it progresses to the point where wolf and dog are shown, as symbols of the animal kingdom. In the foreground it traverses a cultivated field, which symbolizes matters of more or less general knowledge, until it comes to two towers, which mark the boundaries of the known. Then it continues into the Beyond, rising and falling through blue distances which represent the planes of consciousness open to us during sleep or trance.

The towers are the handiwork of man. In the B.O.T.A. version they have battlements. This is because they represent the mental attitude of the average man, who conceives himself to be surrounded by a hostile environment, against which he must fight, and from which he must protect himself. Thus the towers correspond to the mental states symbolized by the hard carapace of the shell-fish.

The path rises and falls, suggesting periodicity, wave-motion, vibration. Yet it continually ascends, so that, as one progresses, the time comes when his most depressed states of consciousness are at a higher level than some of his earlier exaltations.

Key 18 represents the fourth stage of spiritual unfoldment, wherein the knowledge gained by meditation is incorporated into the bodily organism. It is the stage of body-building, or organization in accordance with subconscious mental patterns. In the tableau of major trumps given at the beginning of this outline you will find Key 18 at the bottom of a row of three pictures.

At the top is the Emperor, because reason is the mental tool by which we prepare for right action. In the middle is Justice, representing the law of poised activity, because only by action may we make any progress. At the bottom is the Moon, representing the actual organization of the body-cells. Without organism there can be neither function nor faculty. The unfoldment of our latent powers is made possible by physiological changes in these bodies of flesh and blood.

Thus it is written: "Flesh and blood cannot inherit the kingdom of God," because the changes we speak of are not transmissible from generation to generation. Nature gives us the wild body. Art must perfect it. Yet a flesh and blood body is the necessary vehicle for mastery as expressed here on the physical plane, and though it cannot inherit or transmit the powers of adeptship, it can become a vehicle for those powers when it is rightly organized by adaptive methods.

THE SUN

19   **THE SUN**

XXIII

KEY 19: THE SUN (RESH)

Resh (R, value 200) means the head and face of man. In the head are gathered together, or collected, all the distinctively human powers. The word "countenance," in fact, is derived from a Latin verb meaning "to hold together, to contain." Again, the head of any project is its organizer, director, guiding power, manager, controller. Thus we may expect to find in the symbols of Key 19 plain intimations of authority and leadership.

South, the direction attributed to Resh, is the place of the sun's meridian height, the place of its greatest brilliance and power. On the Cube of Space, this is the southern face, on the observer's right when the cube is viewed from the west.

The Sun is the heavenly body corresponding to Resh. We have found it exalted in Aries (Key 4, The Emperor) and ruling Leo (Key 8, Strength). It is the power which reaches its highest manifestation in reason, and which always and everywhere is the ruling force which makes effective the law symbolized by Strength. The Sun's color is orange. The musical tone is D-natural.

Fruitfulness and Sterility, the pair of opposites attributed to Resh, are the extremes of expression in the manifestation of solar force. The sun causes all growth, but it also makes deserts.

Collecting or *Collective Intelligence* is the mode of consciousness. To collect is to assemble, to bring together, to combine, to unify, to embody, to synthesize. The Collective Intelligence concentrates all the modes of consciousness which have gone before, and combines them together in a new form. Thus it is a regenerative mode of consciousness, incorporating all the elements of control in a new realization of personality.

As the number 19 may be reduced to 10, while 10, in turn, may be reduced to 1, we may understand that the symbolism of the picture now before us is logically dependent on that of the Magician (1) and also on that of the Wheel of Fortune (10). It is also the final term of the series of Keys representing self-conscious intellection, viz., 1, 4, 7, 10, 13 and 16.

The title refers to the dominant symbol, which is a sun with a human countenance. It represents the truth that the seemingly material forces of nature really are modes of a conscious energy, essentially human in character and potencies. The rays of the sun are alternatively waved and salient. The wavy rays represent vibration. The straight ones represent radiation, which is apparently in straight lines.

Four sunflowers, representing the four Qabalistic worlds, and the four kingdoms of nature, mineral, vegetable, animal and human, turn, not toward the day-star, but toward the little children, as if to hint that all creation turns to man for its final development. In the B.O.T.A. version a fifth sunflower is shown. It is still in bud, and turns toward the sun. This bud represents the "Fifth Kingdom," the kingdom of the Spiritual Israel, composed of human beings who, by understanding the law of evolution which has brought organized life-expression as far as ordinary *genus homo*, is enabled to apply that law to the self-evolution of a "new creature," who is as far beyond ordinary humanity as the average human being is beyond the animals. As yet, though the whole line of sages, prophets, adepts and masters belongs to the Fifth Kingdom, that company of new creatures is small, by comparison with the mass of humanity. Thus it is symbolized by a sunflower in bud, rather than in full bloom; and because the outstanding characteristic of all members of the Fifth Kingdom is their utter dependence on the universal Life-power, this fifth flower turns toward the sun.

The wall in the background represents human adaptation of natural conditions. It is, furthermore, a symbol of the whole chain of ideas related to the letter Cheth, because it is a stone fence. Thus it is a symbol of all the ideas represented by Key 7 of Tarot, especially the idea of speech.

Thus Life and the Word (flowers and wall) are shown in the background of Key 19, to indicate the underlying forces at work in what is symbolized by this Key. Note that in the B.O.T.A. version the wall is of stone, in contrast to the bricks which compose the tower in Key 16. Wherever stone appears in Tarot symbolism we are to understand it as a reference to the Hebrew word ABN, Ehben, and thus to the perfect union between the Divine Wisdom which Qabalists call AB, Ab, the Father, and the One Self of the entire human race, which they call BN, Ben, the Son. Human speech (the wall) is actually the manifestation of this union, because all personal consciousness is based on the indissoluble union of the cosmic life-force (Ab, the Father) with the central Self (Ben, the Son) seated in the hearts of men.

From the most primitive speech to the most highly evolved languages, humanity's word-forms evolve as a direct consequence of the fact that the word-maker is the central Self. As that Self evolves higher and higher types of personality, through successive rounds and races, language becomes a more and more adequate vehicle for the expression of ideas. Yet all human language has one basic limitation. Its words are descriptions of, or labels for, various types of sense experience.

Thus the wall, though it is of stone, has five courses, symbolizing the five human senses. Even in the languages which have the largest vocabularies, all concrete terms are limited to describing things and activities within range of the senses, and all abstract terms are derived directly from the field of sensory experience.

This is why language fails whenever one attempts to use it to represent experiences which go beyond the range of physical sensation. This is why mystics and seers are forced to resort to symbolic uses of language. It is not that they are trying to hide anything. Nobody could be more eager to express himself than a wise man who has had first-hand knowledge of the inner and higher planes of experience. This is especially apparent in the writings of the alchemists, who had discovered a Great Secret they wished to share with their fellowmen. Yet none of them succeeded in saying what he saw. To most readers, the alchemists seem to be doing their best to conceal what they know. The truth of the matter is that ordinary speech will not serve to convey this kind of experience from one mind to another.

On the other hand, he who has had the experience finds that he has no difficulty in understanding the words. As one grows into the state of consciousness we have called the Fifth Kingdom, one understands the special meanings which the sages give to words, and discovers that for the seers of all periods of human history there is, so to say, a "new tongue," intelligible to all who have had the higher kind of experience.

Yet even this "magical language" will not serve to express the highest forms of realization. Consequently the children in this Key are shown standing with their backs to the wall, and the little girl, indeed, turns the palm of her hand toward the wall, as if in a gesture of repudiation.

Both children are nude, to show their state of Edenic innocence, comparable to that of the Lovers in Key 6. They are not quite adolescent, to indicate that this stage of unfoldment, though it is one of regeneration, is not the full unfoldment of the powers of the Fifth Kingdom.

The children represent self-consciousness and subconsciousness, and they are dancing in a fairy ring, their hands clasped, to suggest the perfect union and rhythmic synchronization of the activities of the two modes of human personality. Each has one foot planted firmly in the central circle of the ring, so that the other foot is free to swing; and the boy's right hand is extended before him, palm upward, as if ready to accept something he expects to receive.

This Key represents the fifth stage of spiritual unfoldment. It is a degree of adeptship, that of liberation from the limitations of physical matter and circumstances. It is also a grade of conscious self-identification with the One Life. Yet it is not final. For though it is a stage wherein all physical forces are under the control of the adept, who, having himself become childlike, realizes in his own person the fulfilment of the promise, "A little child shall lead them"—yet a person who has reached this grade still feels himself to be a separate, or at least a distinct entity. This is not full liberation, though it is a higher stage than any of those preceding it. It is, in particular, the stage in which all physical forces are dominated by the will of the adept, because he is an unobstructed vehicle for the One Will which always has ruled those forces, since the beginning.

NOTE: Since Key 19 is one in which the symbolism of the B.O.T.A. version, though conforming to that of most other Tarot packs, differs markedly from that of the Rider pack, we feel impelled to close this chapter with the four paragraphs explaining the meaning of the central figure in the symbolism devised by Dr. Waite. We quote from the first edition of: *Key to the Tarot.*

"The child is fair, like the Fool, and like the Fool, wears a wreath and a red feather. The feather has the same meaning as that of the Fool. The wreath is of flowers, instead of leaves, intimating the near approach to the harvest of final realization and liberation.

"The child is naked, in accordance with an old Qabalistic saying that Spirit clothes itself to come down, and divests itself of the garments of matter to go up. The nipples and navel of the child are the points of a water triangle, hinting at the letter Mem and the Hanged Man. For the stage of unfoldment represented by the Sun is the expression of the law the Hanged Man symbolizes.

"His red banner signifies action and vibration. Its black staff is like the black wand of the Fool, but is tipped with a point, similar to the staff of the Charioteer, and like it, signifying concentration. The banner is carried in the left hand as an intimation that the measurement and control of vibration which it indicates has passed from self-consciousness (right hand) to subconsciousness — has become automatic...Thus it is easy, and the great standard seems no burden to the boy.

"He rides a horse, symbol of solar energy, similar to the horse of Death [Key 13 in the Rider pack]. He rides without saddle or bridle, because he represents perfect balance. That balance is maintained by his outstretched right hand, which represents self-consciousness. He is the regenerated personality, recognizing and affirming its unity with the Father, or Source of all. He leaves behind the artificial erections of race-consciousness, and fares forth free and joyous on his journey home."

JUDGEMENT

20 | JUDGEMENT | ש

XXIV

KEY 20: JUDGEMENT (SHIN)

Shin (Sh, value 300) is pronounced "sheen." It means "tooth," probably a serpent's fang, and suggests sharpness, acidity, active manifestation. The number of the letter, 300, is the value of the Hebrew words RVCh ALHIM, Ruach Elohim, which mean "Life-Breath of the Divine Ones," or "Holy Spirit." Therefore do Qabalists call Shin the "Holy Letter."

We may understand this letter as being a symbol of the power which tears down the limitations of form, as teeth break up food. As the serpent's fang, it represents the power which "kills" the false personality and its sense of separateness. Observe that the corresponding Tarot Key is placed below that named Death in the tableau given earlier. In the Cube of Space, Shin corresponds to the inner axis of the cube connecting the center of the northern face with the center of the southern face.

Fire is the element attributed to Shin. It is the particular quality of the solar force and of the Mars vibration. It is also the quality of the zodiacal signs represented in Tarot by the Emperor, Strength and Temperance. Its color is scarlet. The musical tone is C-natural.

Pluto and *Vulcan*, the latter a planet as yet unrecognized by exoteric astronomy, but considered in the calculations of some astrologers, are attributed to Shin.

Perpetual Intelligence is the mode of consciousness. Its name is derived from a Hebrew root meaning "to stretch." This implies that the Perpetual Intelligence is an extension beyond the limits of the modes of consciousness common to most human beings. The name also implies everlastingness, eternity, and thus, conscious immortality.

The number 20 reduces to 2. Thus we understand that the consciousness here represented is the culmination of mental activities originating in the cosmic memory (2, The High Priestess). This picture is the last of the series including Keys 2, 5, 8, 11, 14 and 17.

Judgement, sometimes *The Last Judgement,* is the title of Key 20. It implies completion, decision, termination. It is the final state of personal consciousness, because that which is represented by the Tarot Key following it is a state wherein personal consciousness is wholly obliterated in a higher realization.

Dr. Waite's version of the twentieth trump is less happy than any of his other departures from medieval symbolism. It shows three additional figures in the background, but these add nothing of importance to the real meaning of the design. Thus the B.O.T.A. version, like all other versions of this trump, shows only one group.

They are a man, a woman, and a child. Their bodies are tinted gray, rather than flesh-color, to intimate—1: that in this phase of personal consciousness the "pairs of opposites" have been neutralized, as complementary colors are neutralized in gray; 2: that the scene depicted is not located in the physical plane.

The man is self-consciousness, the woman subconsciousness, and the child the regenerated personality. The positions of their arms refer to the symbolic gestures used in certain occult societies to represent the letters L (woman's extended arms), V (upraised arms of child) and X (crossed arms of man), which spell the Latin noun LVX, meaning "Light."

The angel is the Divine Breath, or cosmic fire, yet he is obviously the angel Gabriel, not only because he carries a trumpet, but also because Gabriel is the angel of the element of water, which is indicated by his blue robe.

The action of heat upon water creates air, the substance of breath. Breath is specialized in sound, and the basis of sound is sevenfold. These seven basic tones are indicated by seven lines radiating from the bell of the trumpet, itself an instrument utilizing sound vibration. What these tones are, and how to employ them, is not material for discussion in this elementary treatise. Suffice to say that sound is the instrument of final liberation, and that the seven tones are those which affect the seven interior stars by sympathetic vibration.

The banner of the cross should measure exactly 5 by 5 units (and does so in the B.O.T.A. version). Thus the arms of the cross will include 9 out of the 25 square units on the face of the banner. 9 is the number of completion, and 5 is the number of adaptation. Complete adaptation is one, but only one, of the esoteric meanings of the banner.

In the astral plane, or fourth dimension, represented by this Key, all things are the reverse of physical conditions. Hence the man is now in a passive attitude, and the woman receives the influences of the angel in her outstretched hands. Note the correspondence of this stretching gesture to the basic meaning of the Hebrew word translated "Perpetual." The child, as we have said, is the regenerated personality, and it also stretches up both arms to their fullest extent.

The coffins float upon a sea which is the final reservoir of those waters which begin in the robe of the High Priestess. The coffins are rectangular, to represent the three dimensions of the physical plane. Standing at right angles, so to say, to these coffins, the three human figures indicate the mathematical definition of the fourth dimension—that which is at right angles to the other three.

Snowy mountains in the background represent the heights of abstract thought. This takes purely mathematical form. Thus the symbolism suggests that what is shown by Key 20 is derived from mathematical considerations.

The child's back is toward us, because he represents return to the Source of all. This card shows the sixth stage of spiritual unfoldment, in which personal consciousness is on the verge of blending with the universal. At this stage, the adept realizes that his personal existence is nothing but the manifestation of the relationship between self-consciousness and subconsciousness. He sees, too, that self-consciousness and subconsciousness are not themselves personal, but are really modes of universal consciousness. Thus he knows that his personality has no separate existence. At this stage his intellectual conviction is confirmed by fourth-dimensional experiences which finally blot out the delusion of separateness forever.

THE WORLD

21　　THE WORLD　　ת

XXV

KEY 21: THE WORLD (TAV)

Tav (Th, sometimes T, value 400) means signature or mark, but the mark is a cross of equal arms, like that on the breast of the High Priestess. This letter is called Tau in the Greek alphabet, and the Egyptian Tau-cross is said to have been a tally for measuring the depth of the Nile, also a square for measuring right angles. Among the Hebrews it was a symbol of salvation (Ezekiel 9:4). Thus it represents salvation from death, and eternal life.

As representing a signature, this letter implies security, guaranty, pledge, and so on. A signature is what makes business instruments valid. The letter Tav therefore indicates the final seal and witness to the completion of the Great Work of liberation.

Center, sometimes called "the palace of holiness in the midst," is the direction attributed to Tav. This palace of holiness is said to "sustain all things." In Qabalistic writings it is said to be Jerusalem or Zion, where man can commune with God.

The Hebrew word for palace is HIKL, Haikal. The numeral value of this word, 65, is also the number of ADNI, Adonai, Lord.

In the Cube of Space, the letter Tav is the interior center, the point where the three co-ordinates which correspond to the three mother letters cross one another. This center is that *point* which is the fifth dimension. In it all spatial relations are united in a single "here," and all time relations in a single "now." The realization of this one point is the culmination of concentration.

Saturn is the planet corresponding to Tav. According to mythology, Saturn ate his own children. He represents that which absorbs its own expressions back into itself. Exoterically, Saturn is the planet of inertia, concreteness, profundity, weight. It shares the rulership of Aquarius (Key 17, The Star) with Uranus (Key 0, The Fool), and is the ruler of Capricorn (Key 15, The Devil). Saturn is exalted in Libra (Key 11, Justice). Thus we have here a power which is active in meditation, which is the source of those apparent limitations which make us seek a way of escape from bondage, and which is expressed in the equilibrated action symbolized by Justice. Saturn's color is indigo, or blue-violet. The musical tone is A-natural.

Dominion and Slavery is the pair of opposites attributed to Tav. Right interpretation of the necessity for limitation in any form of manifested existence is the secret of dominion. Wrong interpretation of the same thing is the cause of our slavery to conditions. The clue to the right understanding is the aphorism, "He who would rule Nature must first obey her laws."

Administrative Intelligence is the mode of consciousness attributed to Tav. This is consciousness of active participation in the cosmic government. It is entry into the kingdom of heaven as a fully enfranchised citizen, charged with full responsibility for the execution of its laws.

The number 21 is connected with 12 and 3. It is also the sum of the numbers from 0 through 6. Compare it with the Keys bearing these numbers. In particular, study Key 21 as the summation of the ideas represented by the series of pictures from 0 through 6. Again, 21 is the culmination of the series of trumps numbered 3, 6, 9, 12, 15 and 18.

The World is the commoner title. Sometimes this Key is named "The Universe," to indicate that the consciousness it represents is not merely terrestrial, but truly cosmic.

The four animals at the corners of the design have been explained in connection with the tenth Key of Tarot. Note, however, that in Key 10 the Bull faces the Lion, but in Key 21 the Bull faces away from the Lion. This is because the Bull corresponds to the last letter of the Tetragrammaton,

IHVH, which symbolizes the physical plane. In cosmic consciousness the closed circuit of successive transformations of energy is, so to say, broken, so that the limitations of the physical plane and its three dimensions no longer bind the consciousness of the adept.

In the Rider pack, the proportions of the ellipse surrounding the dancing figure are incorrect. In older versions, and in the B.O.T.A. Tarot, this ellipse is five units wide and eight units high. This gives a very close approximation to the quadrature of the circle, and is related also to the dimensions of the sides of the vault described in the Rosicrucian *Fama Fraternitatis*. The proportion is derived from the geometrical construction of the hexagram, or figure of two interlaced triangles, shown in the diagram which is the frontispiece of this book.

In the B.O.T.A. version, as in older packs, the ellipse is formed of twenty-two groups of three leaves, eleven groups on either side. These represent the twenty-two forces corresponding to the letters of the Hebrew alphabet and to the Tarot Keys. There are three leaves in each group, because every one of the twenty-two forces has three modes of expression. Any one of these forces may manifest itself in integration, in disintegration, or in equilibration, according to the way in which it is applied. Note that the ellipse is a zero sign, and zero is the numeral symbol of superconsciousness.

The horizontal 8-shaped bindings at the top and bottom of the wreath are like those over the heads of the Magician, and of the woman in Key 8. They have the same meanings. Here they are red, to suggest that the law symbolized by Keys 1 and 8 has been carried into action. The similarity between them, and their positions, suggest the Hermetic axiom, "That which is above is as that which is below."

The dancer represents the merging of self-consciousness with subconsciousness, and the blending of these two with superconsciousness. Occult tradition says that the scarf, violet in color, and shaped like a letter Kaph, conceals the fact that this is an androgyne figure. In this highest form of conscious experience all sense of separate sex is lost, along with the extinction of the sense of separate personality. The Dancer is the All-Father and the All-Mother. She is the Bride, but she is also the Bridegroom. She is the Kingdom and the King, even as Malkuth, the Kingdom, is by Qabalists called the "Bride," but has also the Divine Name ADNI MLK, Adonai Melek, Lord King.

She bears two wands. In the B.O.T.A. version these are spirals. That in the right hand turns clockwise. The one in the left hand turns counter-clockwise. The wands represent the spiral force of the Life-power. That in the right hand symbolizes Involution, the other represents Evolution.

This Key signifies Cosmic Consciousness, or Nirvana. For full descriptions of this state see Dr. Richard Maurice Bucke's *Cosmic Consciousness*, Ali Nomad's book of the same title, Ouspensky's *Tertium Organum*, Jacob Boehme's *Supersensual Life*, William James' *Varieties of Religious Experience*, and the writings of Swami Vivekananda. The central fact of this experience is that he to whom it comes has first-hand knowledge that he is in perfect union with the One Power which is the Pivot and the Source of the whole cosmos. He knows also that through him the governing and directing power of the universe flows out into manifestation.

Words fail to give any adequate idea of this seventh stage of spiritual unfoldment. We must leave it to your intuition to combine the suggestions of the picture with the meanings of the letter Tav. Here is a representation of what you really are, and of what the cosmos really is. The universe is the Dance of Life. The immortal, central Self of you—That is the Eternal Dancer.

XXVI

METHODS OF STUDY

THIS book aims to put into your hands the fundamental knowledge of Tarot symbolism which will enable you to use the Keys intelligently. In the nature of things, it cannot possibly exhaust the subject. One has only to remember that the twenty-two Keys can be arranged—using them all—in no less than 1,124,727,000,777,607,680,000 *different* ways, to see that when one adds to these the innumerable arrangements of groups of two, three, four, five, six or more Keys, the number of combinations is beyond reckoning. So far as any human being is concerned, the combinations of the Keys are practically infinite. Just as all the words in the dictionary are made up of letters of the alphabet, so may the Tarot Keys be arranged to form a limitless number of "words" in the occult speech of pictorial symbolism.

Indeed, one application of the Tarot Keys is to use them for spelling out words in the Hebrew tongue. This does not mean that every word in a Hebrew dictionary has a hidden occult significance. It does mean that many words in the Old Testament, and in technical works of occultism, do reveal their deeper meanings when they are transposed into the corresponding Tarot Keys. This is particularly true of the divine and angelic names in the Hebrew language, and applies also to many Hebrew proper names such as ADM, Adam, ChVH, Eve, QIN, Cain, HBL, Abel, and so on. The names of the twelve tribes of Israel, in particular, offer many striking suggestions when they are spelled out with Tarot Keys.

Such uses of the Tarot, however, are of interest to relatively few persons. Some of them are dealt with in the more advanced courses of instruction of The Builders of the Adytum, Los Angeles, California.

The most important use of Tarot is to evoke thought. By this time you are aware that every one of the Keys corresponds to something in your own make-up. A very little practice will demonstrate to you the fact that Key 1, for example, will help you to develop a keener power of concentration and attention. By looking at Key 2, you will improve your powers of recollection. Key 3 will develop your creative imagination. And so on, through the series.

We recommend, therefore, that you take one Key daily, and look at it for five minutes. When you do so, let it be your intention to employ the time thus spent for the specific purpose of evoking from your inner consciousness the power which corresponds to that Key.

Throughout this book we have noted the colors and the musical tones corresponding to the Hebrew letters. If you will look at something yellow, and intone the note E-natural before you begin to look at Key 1, you will intensify the evocative effect of that Key. Use, for the intonation, a word like the Sanskrit Pranava, AUM, or the Greek mystery-name IAO, which is pronounced ee – ah – oh. Or intone one of the statements of The Pattern on the Trestleboard.

Provide yourself with a loose-leaf notebook. Often, as you are looking at a Key, it will suggest some new idea. Make a note of it immediately. You may also use this book to keep track of information about Hebrew letters, numbers, etc. You will find, now that you have begun this study, that a surprising quantity of information relative to numbers, Hebrew letters, and other matters connected with Tarot will come your way, almost without your seeking it.

Thus you may need, in addition to your notebook, some convenient way to file clippings from magazines and newspapers. The least satisfactory way to preserve these is to paste them in a book. A set of strong manilla envelopes is far better. For practical purposes, envelopes opening on the side are more convenient. In these you may file your clippings, using whatever simple filing system you may in vent. One of the best is to have twenty-two envelopes, one for each Key. Whenever you add a new item to your collection, put it in the proper envelope, and make a note of it on the outside of the envelope.

Remember, you have only begun to learn about Tarot. To have the benefit of this wonderful invention, the Keys must be inside you. This means that you must be able to call up the image of any Key by a simple act of will. When you can do this, Tarot will be part of your very flesh and blood, and then it will begin to effect far-reaching transformations in your thinking, and thus in your living. What is more, all these transformations will be of positive benefit to yourself and others.

In the more advanced work, you will find it greatly to your advantage to be familiar with the diagram of the Tree of Life at the end of this book. It shows, in the circles, the English names of the ten Qabalistic Sephiroth, their numbers, the names of the ten Rosicrucian Grades, and the mystic equations connected with these Grades.

The paths connecting the ten circles are those of the twenty-two letters and their corresponding Keys. Each of these paths corresponds also to the mode of consciousness attributed to its letter, and each path is related to the color mentioned for its letter in this book.

The colors of the Sephiroth are: Crown, White; Wisdom, Gray; Understanding, Black; Mercy, Blue; Severity, Red; Beauty, Yellow; Victory, Green; Splendor, Orange; Foundation, Violet; Kingdom, Citrine, Russet, Olive and Black. The citrine is placed in the upper quarter of the tenth circle, the russet in the quarter at the observer's left, the olive in the quarter at the observer's right, and the black in the lower quarter.

Thus, from the information given in this book, you will be able to make a colored diagram of the Tree. Not every reader will care to do so, but those who do follow out this hint will find it leading to some very interesting discoveries.

Again, since every path connects two circles, the Tarot Key belonging to it may be said to begin in the circle bearing the smaller number, and to end in the circle bearing the larger. Thus Key 0 is on the eleventh Path of Wisdom, beginning in 1, The Crown, and ending in 2, Wisdom. Many clues to the deeper occult meaning of the Keys, and many of the reasons for the symbols used in their composition, may be found by studying the placing of the Tarot on the Tree of Life. Note that in this diagram the numbers of the Keys are placed near the letters, and are distinguished by small letters leading from the letters to the numbers. The other numbers are the numbers of the Paths of Wisdom. In the Qabalah the Sephiroth are called "paths" and so are the letters. Thus there are Thirty-two Paths of Wisdom. The names of the modes of consciousness or intelligence corresponding to the ten Sephiroth will be found in Chapter 2. The names of the modes of consciousness corresponding to the letters are given in subsequent chapters, throughout this book.

XXVII

TAROT DIVINATION

To CARRY OUT the instructions in this chapter, you will need a complete Tarot pack. It does not much matter what the designs may be. A good pack, drawn by Augustus Knapp, was issued some years since by Manly P. Hall. It is no longer available. The French exoteric Tarot is perfectly good for divination, and so is the Rider pack.

Not everyone can use the Tarot for divination. It takes a certain temperament. If one has this temperament, ordinary cards will serve just as well as the Tarot. If one lacks it, the most careful attention to the rules for divination will not produce satisfactory results. There are many other systems for giving "readings" with Tarot cards. We believe this to be one of the best.

This method of divination is not intended for fortune-telling. If you debase it to that purpose, you will cripple yourself spiritually. Its proper application is to the solution of serious questions, for yourself or others.

Before attempting to divine, learn the divinatory meanings of the 78 cards. Do not try divination until you have committed these meanings to memory, because the subconscious response and control of shuffling required for divination necessitate thorough knowledge of the meaning of every picture.

The divinatory meanings of the major trumps are:

0. The Fool. In spiritual matters: Originality, audacity, venturesome quest. In material affairs: Folly, eccentricity, inconsiderate action.

1. The Magician. Constructive power, initiative, skill, subtlety, craft, occult wisdom and power.
2. The High Priestess. All meanings derivable from duality. Fluctuation, reaction, secrets, things hidden, unrevealed future.
3. The Empress. Fruitfulness, beauty, luxury, pleasure, success. Badly placed in a divinatory layout: Dissipation, luxuriousness, sensuality.
4. The Emperor. Stability, power; reason; ambition; oversight; control.
5. The Hierophant. Intuition, teaching, inspiration; marriage, alliance; occult force voluntarily invoked.
6. The Lovers. Attraction, beauty, love. Harmony of inner and outer life.
7. The Chariot. Triumph, victory, and the like.
8. Strength. Action, courage, power, control of the life-force.
9. The Hermit. Wisdom from above, prudence, circumspection.
10. The Wheel of Fortune. Destiny; good fortune; turn for the better.
11. Justice. Strength and force, but arrested, as in the act of judgement. Legal affairs, lawsuits, when the question relates to material affairs.
12. The Hanged Man. In spiritual matters: Wisdom, surrender to the inevitable. In material affairs: Losses, reverses.
13. Death. Contrarieties; sudden change; death.
14. Temperance. Combination, adaptation, economy, management.
15. The Devil. Bondage, materiality, necessity, force, fate.
16. The Tower. Danger, conflict, unforeseen catastrophes, ambition.
17. The Star. Insight; hope; influence over others.
18. The Moon. Voluntary change; deception; hidden enemies.
19. The Sun. Liberation; gain; riches.
20. Judgement. Decision, renewal; determines a matter.
21. The World. Synthesis; success; change of place.

DIVINATORY MEANINGS OF MINOR TRUMPS

WANDS: Ace (1): Energy, strength, enterprise; principle; beginning.
2. Dominion.
3. Established strength.
4. Perfected work.
5. Strife; competition.
6. Victory after strife; gain.

7. Valor; courage in face of difficulties.
8. Activity; swiftness; approach to goal.
9. Preparedness; strength in reserve; victory after opposition.
10. Oppression; burden of ill-regulated power.
KING: Dark man, friendly, ardent; honesty; possible inheritance.
QUEEN: Dark woman, magnetic, friendly. Business success.
KNIGHT: Dark, friendly, young man. Departure. Change of residence.
PAGE: Dark young man. Messenger. Brilliance, courage.

CUPS: Ace (1): Fertility, productiveness, beauty, pleasure.
2. Reciprocity, reflection.
3. Pleasure, liberality, fulfilment, happy issue.
4. Contemplation. Dissatisfaction with material success.
5. Loss in pleasure. Partial loss. Vain regret.
6. Beginning of steady gain, but beginning only. New relations, new environment.
7. Illusionary success. Ideas, designs, resolutions.
8. Abandoned success; instability. Leaving material success for something higher.
9. Material success; physical well-being.
10. Lasting success; happiness to come.
KING: Fair man; calm exterior. Subtle, violent, artistic.
QUEEN: Fair woman; imaginative, poetic. Gift of vision.
KNIGHT: Fair man, Venusian, indolent. Arrival, approach.
PAGE: Fair, studious youth. Reflection. News.

SWORDS: Ace (1): Invoked force; conquest; activity.
2. Balanced force; indecision; friendship.
3. Sorrow, disappointment, tears. Delay, absence, separation.
4. Rest from strife; relief from anxiety; Quietness, rest, rest after illness. NOT a card of death.
5. Defeat, loss, failure, slander, dishonor.
6. Success after anxiety; passage from difficulties; a journey by water.
7. Unstable effort; uncertainty; partial success.
8. Indecision; waste of energy in details; a crisis.
9. Worry; suffering, despair, misery. Loss.
10. Ruin, pain, desolation; sudden misfortune. NOT a card of sudden death. In spiritual matters: End of delusion.
KING: Distrustful, suspicious man. Full of ideas, thoughts and designs. Care, observation, extreme caution.

QUEEN: Widowhood; mourning. A keen, quick, intensely perceptive, subtle woman. Usually fond of dancing.

KNIGHT: Active, clever, subtle, skilful, domineering young man. Enmity, wrath, war.

PAGE: Vigilant, acute, subtle, active youth.

PENTACLES: Ace (1): Material gain, wealth, contentment.

2. Harmony in midst of change.
3. Construction; material increase; growth; financial gain.
4. Earthly power; physical forces; skill in directing them.
5. Concordance; affinity; adaptation. (Waite's symbolism shows that the concord and harmony are necessarily *interior*. The unfortunates out in the snow are the profane, those who have not grasped the inner light.)
6. Material prosperity, philanthropy, presents.
7. Success unfulfilled; delay, but growth.
8. Skill in material affairs.
9. Prudence; material gain; completion.
10. Wealth; riches; material prosperity.

KING: Friendly, steady, reliable married man.

QUEEN: Generous, intelligent, charming, moody married woman.

KNIGHT: Laborious, patient, dull young man.

PAGE: Diligent, careful, deliberate youth.

N.B. Pages may be young girls as well as young lads. Queens are not *always* married, but represent rather women with experience of life.

1. Before beginning to divine, be sure that the Querent (person for whom divination is made) has formulated his question. Explain to him that all questions come under four major heads — (a) work, business, etc.; (b) love, marriage, or pleasure; (c) trouble, loss, scandal, quarreling, etc.; (d) money, goods and such purely material matters. Be careful that the Querent does not tell you his question or its nature before you begin to divine.

2. Make your mind as passive as possible while you are shuffling and laying out the cards. Do not try to guess. Go by what the cards suggest to you.

3. Do not limit yourself to the divinatory meanings

given in the outline. They are general, and under the special circumstances of a divination, may be altered. Say what comes to you to say.

4. It is better to learn the meanings of the cards than to write the meanings on them. Better for yourself, and more impressive for the Querent. By learning the meanings of three cards a day, you may master the significance of the whole pack in 26 days.

In addition to the meanings given above, observe and learn the following additional points:

Kings and Queens usually show actual men and women connected with the matter.

Knights sometimes represent the coming or going of a matter, according to the direction in which they face.

Pages indicate young people, but often show opinions, thought, ideas – either in harmony with, or opposed to the subject.

A majority of:

WANDS – Energy, opposition, quarrel.
CUPS – Pleasure, merriment.
SWORDS – Trouble, sadness, sickness, death.
PENTACLES – Business, money, possessions.
MAJOR TRUMPS – Strong forces beyond the Querent's control.
COURT CARDS – Society, meetings of many persons.
ACES – Strength generally. Aces are always strong cards.

If a spread contains:

4 Aces – Great power and force.
3 Aces – Riches, success.
4 Knights – Swiftness, rapidity.
3 Knights – Unexpected meetings. Knights, as a rule, show news.
4 Queens – Authority and influence.
3 Queens – Powerful friends.
4 Kings – Meetings with the great.
3 Kings – Rank and honor.
4 Pages – New ideas or plans.
3 Pages – Society of the young.
4 Tens – Anxiety, responsibility.

3 Tens – Buying, selling, commerce.
4 Nines – Added responsibilities.
3 Nines – Correspondence.
4 Eights – Much news.
3 Eights – Much journeying.
4 Sevens – Disappointments.
3 Sevens – Compacts, contracts.
4 Sixes – Pleasure.
3 Sixes – Gain, success.
4 Fives – Order, regularity.
3 Fives – Quarrels, fights.
4 Fours – Rest, peace.
3 Fours – Industry.
4 Threes – Resolution, determination.
3 Threes – Deceit.
4 Twos – Conferences, conversations.
3 Twos – Reorganization, recommendation.

A card is strong or weak, well dignified or ill dignified according to the cards next to it on either side. Cards of the same suit on either side strengthen it greatly for good or evil, according to their nature. Cards of opposite natures weaken it greatly, for either good or evil.

Swords are inimical to Pentacles; Wands are inimical to Cups. Swords are friendly with Cups and Wands; Wands are friendly with Swords and Pentacles.

If a card falls between two others which are inimical to each other (as a Sword card between a Cup and a Wand), it is not much affected by either.

METHOD OF DIVINATION

1. *The Significator.*–This is the card selected to represent the Querent.

Married Men – Kings.
Bachelors – Knights.
Women Past 18 – Queens.
Adolescents of Either Sex – Pages.

Some diviners use the Magician for men, the High Priestess for women. Others choose the major trump representing the sun sign of the Querent, on the hypothesis that the sun sign represents the true individuality of the person. In general, however, it is safer to choose one of the sixteen court cards, as indicated above. Choose the Significator according to your knowledge or judgement of the Querent's character, rather than according to his physical characteristics.

2. Shuffle the cards, until you feel like stopping.

3. Hand the cards to Querent, ask him to think of the question attentively, and cut the cards with his left hand. The Querent should restore the cut, that is, put the pile which was on the bottom before cutting above the pile consisting of the upper half of the pack.

4. Take the cards as cut, and place them on the table before you.

5. Cut the pack with the left hand, and place the top half to the left.

6. Cut each of these two packs to the left.

7. These four stacks represent IHVH from right to left.

8. Find the Significator. If in the I pack, the question refers to work, enterprise ideas, etc.; if in the H pack, to marriage, love or pleasure; if in the V pack to trouble, loss, scandal, quarreling, etc.; if in the second H pack, to money, goods, purely material matters.

9. Tell the Querent what he has come for. That is, from the position of the Significator in one of the 4 piles, declare to him the general nature of his question. If wrong, abandon the divination. Do not resume the attempt within two hours. Better, wait until another day.

10. If right, spread out the pack containing the Significator, arranging the cards in a circle or wheel.

11. Count the cards from the Significator, in the direction in which the figure printed on card faces. If the figure on the card faces neither right nor left, but straight out from the picture, count to your left.

N.B.—It is advisable to arrange the cards on the table so that the Significator will be at the top of the wheel. But be careful not to alter the sequence of the cards in so doing.

The counting should invariably include the card from which you start. Thus, if the Significator is a Page, you will count Seven, and if the card the count ends with be a seven in one of the suits of minor trumps, you will begin your second count of seven with that card and so on.

For Kings, Queens and Knights, count 4.

For Pages, count 7.

For Aces, count 11.

For small cards of minor trumps, count according to the number printed at the top.

For major trumps, count: 3 for elemental trumps (0, FOOL; 12, HANGED MAN; 20, JUDGEMENT); 9 for the planetary trumps (those corresponding to double letters and pairs of opposites); 12 for trumps representing signs of the zodiac.

Make a story of these cards. It is the story of the beginning of the affair.

12. Pair the cards on either side of the Significator, then those outside them, and so on. Make another story, filling up details omitted in the first.

These two stories may not be quite accurate, but it is to be remembered that your Querent does not, as a rule, know everything about the matter. Nevertheless, the main outlines should be such as he can recognize. If not, abandon the operation at this point.

SECOND OPERATION

Develops the question.

1. Shuffle and let Querent cut, as before.

2. Deal the cards into 12 packs, for the 12 astrological houses of heaven.

3. Find the Significator. According to house in which it is found, judge that the matter will be affected by the general quality of that house. The meanings of the houses are:

First—The person himself.

Second—His finances. Gain or loss, according to the cards found in this pile.

Third—Brothers, sisters. Short journeys, writings, mental inclinations and abilities.

Fourth—Father, home, environment, domestic affairs, lands, mines and real estate generally.

Fifth—Children, love affairs, pleasure, speculation.

Sixth—Sickness, servants, employers, food, clothing, hygiene, service, small animals.

Seventh—Unions, partnership, marriage, contracts, dealings with others, and the public generally, legal affairs, open enmities.

Eighth—Death, psychic experiences of the spiritistic kind, all matters connected with the dead, such as legacies, etc. Also financial affairs of the business or marriage partner.

Ninth—Long journeys, foreign countries, places remote from birthplace, philosophy, religion, education, dreams, visions, psychic development.

Tenth—Profession, occupation, honor, fame, promotion, mother, employer. Also government affairs.

Eleventh—Friends, associations, hopes and fears.

Twelfth—Unseen or unexpected troubles, hidden or secret enmities. Restraint, limitations, hospitals, prisons, insane asylums, sanitariums and the like. Secret societies, occultism of the practical sort, and organizations devoted to it. Large animals.

4. Spread out the pile containing the Significator, as in former operation, and count and pair as before. Remember that the two stories thus developed must be more or less colored by the nature of the house in which the Significator falls.

THIRD OPERATION

1. Shuffle, etc., as before.

2. Deal cards into twelve stacks, representing the signs of the zodiac. Even if you have no astrological information particularly, you can judge the general meaning of the signs, because each is represented by a major trump. For example, if the Significator should fall in the stack corresponding to Capricorn, the further development of the question would be in accordance with the occult meaning of the letter Ayin and the 15th major trump. If a material question, it would probably denote limitation. If one of pleasure, danger or over-indulgence on the sense side. Your own knowledge of the trumps will help you in this.

The order of the 12 signs is:

1. Aries — 4. EMPEROR
2. Taurus — 5. HIEROPHANT
3. Gemini — 6. LOVERS
4. Cancer — 7. CHARIOT
5. Leo — 8. STRENGTH
6. Virgo — 9. HERMIT
7. Libra — 11. JUSTICE
8. Scorpio — 13. DEATH
9. Sagittarius — 14. TEMPERANCE
10. Capricorn — 15. DEVIL
11. Aquarius — 17. STAR
12. Pisces — 18. MOON

3. Find Significator, count and pair as before.

FOURTH OPERATION

1. Shuffle, etc., as before.
2. Deal cards into ten stacks. Each stack corresponds to one of the Sephiroth, and thus to one of the statements of being in the B.O.T.A. affirmations. Thus, if the Significator should fall in the seventh pile, the conclusions of the divination would all be colored by the statement "Living from that Will, supported by its unfailing Wisdom and Understanding, mine is the Victorious life," and your advice to the Querent would all proceed from that basic idea.
3. Find Significator, count and pair as before.

As a rule, but not always, the first operation shows past time, particularly in the pairing of cards, when those which are in the pile away from which the Significator faces will usually indicate past time. If he faces out, those on your right will be past time as a rule.

Experience alone will enable you to judge time with any degree of accuracy, and no rules can be given. If you are possessed of the psychic qualifications necessary to a diviner, you will "feel" time.

Finally, let me reiterate the thought that this is not to be used for vulgar fortune telling, or to amuse a party of friends. If you yield to the temptation so to abuse this information, you will pay for it in the loss of all power of true divination, and probably in the loss of ability to control the higher rates of psychic vibration. Thus the ultimate result of abuse of this divinatory practice will be to make you more negative, more the slave of circumstance, more liable to evil of every kind.

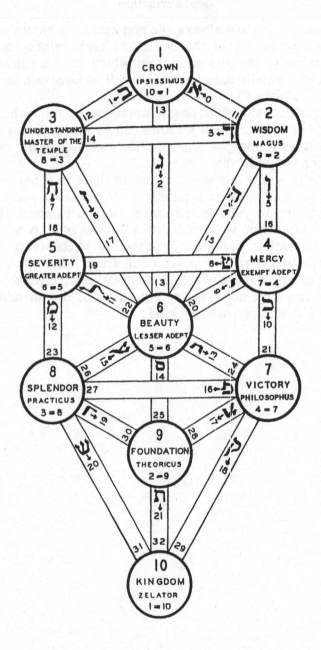

RESOURCES

Paul Foster Case worked extensively with the Hebrew language and with the system of gematria, a language that derives meaning from the numeric value of each Hebrew letter. For those interested in furthering their knowledge of Hebrew, available resources include:

Builders of the Adytum. *The Hebrew Letter Workbook.* Los Angeles: Builders of the Adytum, 1992.
Paul Foster Case. *Highlights of Tarot.* Los Angeles: Builders of the Adytum, 1984.
Jay P. Green, ed. and trans. *The Interlinear Bible.* Peabody, MA: Hendrickson Publishers, 2005.
James Orr, ed. *The International Standard Bible Encyclopedia.* Peabody, MA: Hendrickson Publishers, 2002.
James Strong. *The Exhaustive Concordance of the Bible.* Peabody, MA: Hendrickson Publishers, 1988.

Other works by Paul Foster Case include:

The Book of Tokens, Tarot Meditations. Los Angeles: Builders of the Adytum, 1989.
Daniel, Master of Magicians and The Name of Names. Los Angeles: Builders of the Adytum, 1995.
The Great Seal of the United States. Los Angeles: Builders of the Adytum, 1976.
The Masonic Letter G. Richmond, VA: McCoy Publishing, 1981.
The True and Invisible Rosicrucian Order. York Beach, ME: Weiser, 1989.

Further works of interest include:

Ann Davies. *Inspirational Thoughts on the Tarot*. Los Angeles: Builders of the Adytum, 1997.
———. *Keeping the Outer Temple: Principles of Health and Diet*. Los Angeles: Builders of the Adytum, 1993.
———. *This Is the Truth About the Self*. Los Angeles: Builders of the Adytum, 1974.
Jason Lotterhand. *The Thursday Night Tarot*. North Hollywood, CA: Newcastle Publishing, 1989.

A complete catalogue of books, tapes, CDs, and materials related to the study of the Tarot and other esoteric subjects is available from Builders of the Adytum at www.bota.org.

INDEX

Index

ABOUT THE AUTHOR

Paul Foster Case (1884–1954) was a world-renowned authority on Tarot and Qabalah and the founder of Builders of the Adytum (B.O.T.A.). Born in Fairport, New York, Case became interested in theater at an early age and was an accomplished musician.

His interest in Tarot began at the turn of the twentieth century, ignited by a question from occult scholar Claude Bragdon, who asked: "Case, where do you suppose playing cards came from?" Case's inquisitive mind led him to the study of the Tarot and thus to occultism, for which he had been prepared by an early interest in psychology. His first work on Tarot appeared in *The Word* magazine; this was followed by a series of articles in *Azoth*. Case succeeded Michael Whitty as director of the latter magazine.

In the late 1910s, Case became Praemonstrator General (Supreme Chief) of the occult organization Hermetic Order of the Golden Dawn for the United States and Canada. Leaving the Golden Dawn several years later, Case in 1922 founded the organization that would become Builders of the Adytum, which dedicated itself to the study of practical occultism. At this time Case began actively lecturing on and teaching Tarot and related subjects. He published *The Book of Tokens*, a volume of meditations on Tarot and its corresponding Hebrew letters, which contained material Case received together with Michael Whitty.

Case continued writing extensively on Tarot, Qabalah, Rosicrucianism, alchemy, magic, and the correlation of color and sound in healing. He and his wife, Harriet, along with the Reverend Ann Davies, worked closely together for many years. After Case's death in Los Angeles in 1954, Mrs. Case continued to work with Rev. Davies in forwarding the efforts of Builders of the Adytum.

Case left behind some of the most penetrating studies of Tarot, Qabalah, and related subject matter. He regarded his 1947 volume, *The Tarot*, as his magnum opus on the subject.

In addition to his studies of the occult, Case was an accomplished student of legerdemain (or sleight of hand), and was a member of the International Brotherhood of Magicians and the International Guild of Prestidigitators. Case was also a member of the Liberal Catholic Church.

ABOUT B.O.T.A.

Builders of the Adytum (B.O.T.A.) is a nonprofit, international religious organization whose major objective is promoting the welfare of humanity through the realization of the potential inherent in every human being, using the methods of the Western Mystery Tradition. *Adytum* is Greek for "Inner Shrine."

B.O.T.A. offers correspondence lessons in the principles and practices of Tarot, Qabalah, Spiritual Alchemy, Occult Psychology, Astrology, and the esoteric meaning and uses of sound and color. Lessons are available in Spanish, French, and German, as well as English.

For more information, contact B.O.T.A. at www.bota.org, or at Builders of the Adytum, 5101 North Figueroa Street, Los Angeles, CA 90042.